EVIDENCE
THAT DEMANDS
A VERDICT

STUDY GUIDE | SIX SESSIONS

JESUS AND THE GOSPELS

JOSH MCDOWELL
& SEAN MCDOWELL, PHD

Harper*Christian*
Resources

Evidence That Demands a Verdict Study Guide
© 2019 by Josh McDowell & Sean McDowell, PhD

Requests for information should be addressed to:
HarperChristian Resources, 3900 Sparks Dr. SE, Grand Rapids, Michigan 49546

ISBN 978-0-310-09672-6 (softcover)
ISBN 978-0-310-09673-3 (ebook)

Contents

Introduction

Welcome to the *Evidence That Demands a Verdict* Bible study. For the next six sessions, we will be investigating some of the most important questions we can ask in life. Questions such as:

- Why is evidence important for faith?
- Is there such a thing as truth?
- Is the New Testament reliable?
- Did Jesus actually rise from the dead?
- Did Jesus claim to be God?
- How do we know the Bible is accurate?

It's a big journey that we are undertaking—a journey that for me (Josh) began as a result of a struggle. I started my college years with a lot of hurt, anger, and bitterness. I was desperately seeking happiness and meaning in life, and I simply didn't know where to find it. I was successful in school, in business, in sports, and even in campus leadership. I put on a smile and acted like I had it all together, but my life seemed so empty. I desperately wanted to know truth.

It was at college that I encountered a small group of people, two professors or three professors and eight students, whose lives I could tell were different. It was clear to me they had something I didn't have. So, one day I asked one of the professors, "Tell me why you're so different from all the other students and faculty." She looked me straight in the eye and said two words I never expected to hear: "Jesus Christ."

Her answer struck me as the stupidest thing I had ever heard. "Jesus Christ?" I laughed. "Don't give me that kind of garbage. I'm fed up with religion and the Bible. And I'm fed up with the church." Immediately, she shot back, "Mister, I didn't say *religion*. I said *Jesus Christ*." She pointed out something I had not known—Christianity is *not* a religion. Christianity is God coming to men and women *through* Jesus Christ.

My new friends then issued me a challenge. They dared me—a pre-law student—to make a rigorous and intellectual examination of the claims of Jesus Christ. At first I thought it was a joke, but eventually I accepted their challenge. In time, the evidence led me to the conclusion that God did manifest himself through the Scriptures and the person of Christ. But what brought me to Christ was the love of God. I saw in the Bible that even if I were the only person in the world, Jesus would *still* have died for me.

Once I came to this intellectual conviction, I began to strategize how I could share the things I had discovered with others. During the first thirteen years after becoming a Christian, I shared my faith and continued to research the evidential basis for the Christian faith. After I would speak, people from the audience would ask me for copies of my notes. This gave me the idea of publishing my research to inform those who were truly seeking truth as well as to encourage followers of Christ. Out of this work came *Evidence That Demands a Verdict*.

Each video session in this study will feature a fifteen- to twenty-minute discussion between me and my son Sean as we tackle some of the biggest challenges to Christianity that we present in the book. During the course of this study, you will receive a background in what is known as *apologetics*. Note that this word does not mean to *apologize* for your faith—rather, it comes from the Greek word *apologia*, which means "to answer" or "to reason." In other words, if someone asks why you believe in Jesus, the answer your give them is apologetics.

Christianity does not demand a *blind* faith but an *intelligent* faith. To this end, this study will help you to know the truth, understand your faith, and provide sound evidence to enable you to defend your beliefs. But even more, it will help you remember the reason *why* it is important to do this—not to get into intellectual arguments and prove a point but so you can share the love and truth of God with others. The core of apologetics, and this study, is about clearing away the stumbling blocks that derail people from their journey to Christ.

If you are a follower of Christ, our prayer is that God will use this material to give you newfound confidence that what you believe is true and a newfound ability to boldly share your faith with others. And if you are one who is seeking to know more about Christ, our prayer is that you will discover through this study just how much God truly cares for you and desires to know you personally. So, with this in mind . . . let's begin!

Josh McDowell

How to Use
This Guide

The *Evidence That Demands a Verdict* video study is designed to be experienced in a group setting such as a Bible study, Sunday school class, or any small group gathering. Each session begins with a welcome section, two questions to get you thinking about the topic, and a reading from a key passage of Scripture. You will then watch a fifteen- to twenty-minute video featuring Josh McDowell and Sean McDowell and engage in some small-group discussion. You will close each session with a brief time of personal reflection and prayer as a group.

Each person in the group should have his or her own copy of this study guide. You are also encouraged to have a copy of *Evidence That Demands a Verdict*, as reading the book alongside the curriculum will provide you with deeper insights and make the journey more meaningful. (See the Recommended Reading section at the end of each between-studies section for the chapters that correspond to material you and your group are discussing.)

To get the most out of your group experience, keep the following points in mind. First, the real growth in this study will happen during your small-group time. This is where you will process the content of the teaching, ask questions, and learn from others as you hear what God is doing in their lives. For this reason, it is important for you to be fully committed to the group and attend each session so you can build trust and rapport with the other members. If you choose to only go through the motions, or if you refrain from participating, there is a lesser chance you will find what you're looking for during this study.

Second, remember the goal of your small group is to serve as a place where people can share, learn about God, and build intimacy and friendship. For this reason, seek to make your group a safe place. This means being honest about your thoughts and feelings and listening carefully to everyone else's opinion.

Third, resist the temptation to fix a problem someone might be having or to correct his or her theology, as that's not the purpose of your small-group time. Also, keep everything your group shares confidential. This will foster a rewarding sense of community in your group and create a place where people can heal, be challenged, and grow spiritually.

Following your group time, reflect on the material you have covered by engaging in any or all of the between-sessions activities. For each session, you may wish to complete the personal study all in one sitting or spread it out over a few days (for example, working on it a half-hour a day on different days that week). Note that if you are unable to finish (or even start) your between-sessions personal study, you should still attend the group study video session. You are still wanted and welcome at the group even if you don't have your "homework" done.

Keep in mind that the videos, discussion questions, and activities are simply meant to kick-start your imagination—so you are not only open to what God wants you to hear but also how to apply it to your life. As you go through this study, be attentive to what God is saying to you as you weigh the *evidence that demands a verdict* for Jesus and the Gospels.

Note: If you are a group leader, there are additional resources provided in the back of this guide to help you lead your group members through the study.

WHY IS EVIDENCE IMPORTANT FOR FAITH?

[God] has saved us and called us with a holy calling,
not according to our works, but according to His own purpose and
grace which was given to us in Christ Jesus . . . to which I was
appointed a preacher, an apostle, and a teacher of the Gentiles. . . .
I know whom I have believed and am persuaded that He is able to
keep what I have committed to Him until that Day.

2 TIMOTHY 1:9, 11–12

Welcome

Imagine a courtroom scene. At the head of the courtroom, behind a desk on an elevated platform, sits the judge. Positioned nearby is the court reporter, the clerk, and the bailiff. To the right is the jury. In the middle of the room, off to one side, is the lawyer who will be prosecuting the case. To the other side is the defendant and his attorney.

It is the job of the prosecutor to make his case in such a way that it leaves no reasonable doubt the defendant is guilty. To do so, he will call witnesses to testify and present relevant evidence. But now imagine that as the prosecutor steps up to make his opening arguments, he simply tells the judge and jury that they need to have faith that his convictions about the defendant are true. Chances are, not only would the prosecutor fail in his attempts to get the court to believe him in "blind faith," but he would also likely get thrown off the case.

What is interesting is that many Christians today treat their faith this same way. Some even believe this type of blind faith is *required* . . . that they are never supposed to have any doubts about God, or the Bible, or the doctrines they learned in church. German philosopher and atheist Friedrich Nietzsche criticized Christians for this very reason when he wrote, "Christianity has done its utmost to close the circle and declared even doubt to be sin. One is supposed to be cast into belief without reason, by a miracle, and from then on to swim in it as in the brightest and least ambiguous of elements. . . . What is wanted are blindness and intoxication and an eternal song over the waves in which reason has drowned."[1]

The truth is that Christianity never demands blind faith. Furthermore, by taking on the role of the prosecutor and investigating the claims of the Bible, we find that God *does* provide enough evidence for rational belief. In fact, author Lee Strobel, a former journalist and skeptic, found after conducting his own investigation of Christianity, "The conclusion was compelling, an intelligent entity has quite literally spelled out the evidence of his existence through the four chemical letters in the genetic code. It's almost as if the Creator autographed every cell."[2]

God has not provided *exhaustive* knowledge of his existence, but he has given *sufficient* knowledge for those with an open heart and mind. In this session, we will take the first step on this journey to discovery by looking at why evidence is so important for faith.[3]

Share

If you or any of your group members are just getting to know one another, take a few minutes to introduce yourselves. Next, begin by discussing one of the following questions:

- Why is it important to have evidence to back up your belief in something? When are some times that you put your faith in something that later proved to not be worthy of your trust?

— or —

- What is the single biggest question about truth, the Bible, or Jesus that you find people struggle with today? What evidence are you hoping God provides to you during this study to answer that question?

Read

Invite someone to read aloud the following passage from 1 Peter 3:15–17. Listen for fresh insight and then share any new thoughts with the group using the questions that follow.

Sanctify the Lord God in your hearts, and always be ready to give a defense to everyone who asks you a reason for the hope that is in you, with meekness and fear; having a good conscience, that when they defame you as evildoers, those who revile your good conduct in Christ may be ashamed. For it is better, if it is the will of God, to suffer for doing good than for doing evil.

According to this passage, what should believers in Christ be ready to defend?

What traits should you display when sharing the evidence for your faith?

Which of these two is harder for you to maintain when you are in the midst of defending your beliefs? Why?

Watch

Play the video for session one. As you watch, use the following outline to record any thoughts or concepts that stand out to you.

Notes

What apologetics is all about is clearing away the stumbling blocks that people have on their journey to Christ. It is a way of loving other people.

Christianity is a historical and testable faith. One thing that separates Christianity from other religions is that it is based on truth. If you follow the evidence, it will lead you to truth.

The Bible does not teach that you should have blind faith. Rather, the biblical pattern is that God does some kind of miracle or reveals himself, which gives people knowledge, and then they are called to exercise an examined and intelligent faith in him.

Apologetics simply means to be ready at all times to give a reason for the hope that you have found in God, the Scriptures, and the Christian story.

Apologetics is not a recent phenomenon in the church. Jesus reasoned with people, as did the apostle Paul and many of the first- and second-century church fathers.

Today, the internet has brought many challenges to the Christian faith, but it has also brought awareness to the great amount of historical evidence that reveals Christianity is true.

. . . .

FIVE REASONS WHY APOLOGETICS
IS IMPORTANT TODAY

1. *We are all apologists anyway:* Apologetics is not listed as a spiritual gift for teachers, preachers, or evangelists, as though only some ought to become apologists. Rather, all Christians are called to be ready with an answer.

2. *Apologetics strengthens believers:* When Christians learn good evidences for the truth of the Bible, for the existence of God, or how to respond to tough challenges to the faith, they gain confidence in their beliefs.

3. *Apologetics helps students hang on to their faith:* Young people today have genuine intellectual questions—including questions about their faith. When these questions are not answered, many leave the church.

4. *Apologetics helps with evangelism:* One of the key functions of apologetics is to respond to peoples' questions and clear away any objections or doubts they have that hinder their trust in Christ.

5. *Apologetics helps shape culture:* Apologetics questions come from both Christians and non-Christians—because they both live in the same cultures, and the same world influences their thinking.[4]

. . . .

Discuss

Take a few minutes with your group members to discuss what you just watched and explore these concepts in Scripture.

1. Did you grow up in a church and family environment where you were told what to believe or in one where everything was questioned? How has this environment in which you were raised affected how you approach your faith in Christ today?

2. Why is it important to know *why* you believe rather than just *what* you believe?

3. Paul wrote, "Do your best to present yourself to God as one approved, a worker who does not need to be ashamed and who correctly handles the word of truth" (2 Timothy 2:15 NIV). What are practical ways you can "correctly handle the word of truth" today?

4. Why do you think popular culture (and even many Christians) embrace "blind faith"? What are some of the problems with this approach to faith?

5. What is the difference between *intelligent* faith and *blind* faith? Based on the words of 1 Peter 3:15, which do you think Scripture teaches you to pursue?

6. How can knowing the evidence behind what you believe about Christ help you to remove any stumbling blocks that others might have in their journey toward faith in Jesus?

Respond

Theologian Clark Pinnock described apologetics as being "an activity of the Christian mind which attempts to show that the gospel message is true in what it affirms . . . an apologist is one who is prepared to defend the message against criticism and distortion, and to give evidences of its credibility."[5] As noted in the teaching, apologetics is not a recent phenomenon in the church. In fact, there are at least eight instances in the New Testament where the writers employed the Greek word *apologia,* which is often translated in English as "defense." Today, close out your time by selecting two verses from the list below that use this word. Briefly read over the corresponding passage and write down what the person was "defending" in each case.

Verse	Passage	What the Person Was Defending
Acts 22:1: "Brethren and fathers, hear my *defense* before you now."	Acts 22:1–21	

Verse	Passage	What the Person Was Defending
Acts 25:16: "It is not the custom . . . to hand over any man before the accused . . . has an opportunity to make his *defense*" (NASB)	Acts 25:13–21	
1 Corinthians 9:3: "My *defense* to those who examine me is this . . ."	1 Corinthians 9:1–12	
1 Corinthians 7:11: "For observe . . . that you sorrowed in a godly manner: What diligence it produced in you, what *clearing of yourselves*."	2 Corinthians 7:8–12	
Philippians 1:7: "I have you in my heart, inasmuch as both in my chains and in the *defense* and confirmation of the gospel."	Philippians 1:3–8	

Verse	Passage	What the Person Was Defending
Philippians 1:15–16: "Some indeed preach Christ . . . from goodwill . . . knowing that I am appointed for the *defense* of the gospel."	Philippians 1:15–18	
2 Timothy 4:16: "At my first *defense* no one stood with me, but all forsook me."	2 Timothy 4:9–16	
1 Peter 3:15: "Always be ready to give a *defense* to everyone who asks you a reason for the hope that is in you."	1 Peter 3:13–17	

Pray

Wrap up your time by taking a few moments to pray together. Here are a few ideas of what you could pray about based on the topics of this session:

- Ask God to give you a hunger and a joy to know truth.
- Express your willingness to pursue the evidence for your beliefs . . . wherever that might lead.
- Pray for the courage to pursue an *intelligent* faith over a *blind* faith.
- Tell God your desire for answers to the big questions with which you are struggling.

BETWEEN-SESSIONS
PERSONAL STUDY

Reflect on the material you've covered this week by engaging in any or all of the following between-sessions activities. Each day offers a short reading from *Evidence That Demands a Verdict*, along with a few reflection questions to take you deeper into the theme of this week's study. This week, before you begin this study, you may wish to review the Introduction, Prologue, "He Changed My Life" section, and chapter 1 in *Evidence That Demands a Verdict*. Be sure to journal or write down your thoughts after each question. At the start of the next session, you will have a few minutes to share any insights you learned.

Was Jesus an Apologist?
Evidence That Demands a Verdict, page xxxiii

As you saw in the teaching for this week, all of the New Testament appearances of the word *apologia*—with the exception of 1 Peter 3:15—come from the writing or the ministry of the apostle Paul. The Gospels do not mention Jesus using the word *apologia*, nor is that word employed in their descriptions of how he taught the people. Nevertheless, a strong case can be made that Jesus was, indeed, an apologist.

Douglas Groothuis, a professor of philosophy, has carefully studied the question of whether Jesus was a philosopher, an apologist, or both. In an article published in the *Christian Research Journal*, he provides many examples of how Jesus rationally defended the crucial claims of Christianity, and then concludes:

Contrary to the views of critics, Jesus Christ was a brilliant thinker, who used logical arguments to refute His critics and establish the truth of His views. When Jesus praised the faith of children, He was encouraging humility as a virtue, not irrational religious trust or a blind leap of faith in the dark. Jesus deftly employed a variety of reasoning strategies in His debates on various topics. These include escaping the horns of a dilemma, *a fortiori* arguments,[6] appeals to evidence, and *reductio ad absurdum* arguments.[7]

Jesus' use of persuasive arguments demonstrates that He was both a philosopher and an apologist who rationally defended His worldview in discussions with some of the best thinkers of His day. This intellectual approach does not detract from His divine authority but enhances it. Jesus' high estimation of rationality and His own application of arguments indicates that Christianity is not an anti-intellectual faith. Followers of Jesus today, therefore, should emulate His intellectual zeal, using the same kinds or arguments He Himself used. Jesus' argumentative strategies have applications to four contemporary debates: the relationship between God and morality, the reliability of the New Testament, the resurrection of Jesus, and ethical relativism.[8]

Read Matthew 23:23–33. The term "horns of a dilemma" refers to two choices that both have difficult or unpleasant outcomes. Throughout the New Testament, the Jewish religious leaders tried to trap Jesus in these types of dilemmas. How did Jesus escape the trap the Sadducees tried to set for him in this passage? How did Jesus *defend* his position?

Do you see Jesus more as a philosopher, apologist, or a combination of the two? Why?

Read John 7:14–19. How did Jesus use apologetics in his teaching in this passage?

Some would argue Christianity is anti-intellectual faith. How does Jesus prove otherwise?

According to Groothuis, the strategies Jesus used can apply to four contemporary debates: (1) *the relationship between God and morality*, (2) *the reliability of the New Testament*, (3) *the resurrection of Jesus*, and (4) *ethical relativism (the belief that morality is relative to what is considered moral or immoral in a given culture)*. Which of these four categories do you feel most—and least—qualified to speak on? Why?

❷ We Are All Apologists
Evidence That Demands a Verdict, pages xxxiii–xxxiv

In Paul's letters, he provides two separate lists of the "gifts of the Spirit" (see Romans 12:6–8; 1 Corinthians 12:4–11,:28) and one listing the offices within the church (see Ephesians 4:11). Paul does not include apologetics in any of these lists as a spiritual gift for teachers, preachers, or evangelists. Rather, *all* Christians are called to be apologists—those who are ready with an answer to defend their faith (see 1 Peter 3:15; Jude 3).

Beyond the specific Christian calling to have a ready defense for the faith, there is a sense in which everyone is already an apologist for *something*. In fact, the question is not *whether* we are apologists, but *what kind* of apologists we are. Christian author and social critic Os Guinness addresses this idea when he writes:

> From the shortest texts and tweets to the humblest website, to the angriest blog, to the most visited social networks, the daily communications of the wired world attest that everyone is now in the business of relentless self-promotion—presenting themselves, explaining themselves, defending themselves, selling themselves or sharing their inner thoughts and emotions as never before in human history. That is why it can be said that we are in the grand secular age of apologetics. The whole world has taken up apologetics without ever knowing the idea as Christians understand it. We are all apologists now, if only on behalf of "the Daily Me" or "the Tweeted Update" that we post for our virtual friends and our cyber community. The great goals of life, we are told, are to gain the widest possible public attention and to reach as many people in the world with our products—and always, our leading product is Us.[9]

Think about the statement, "Everyone is already an apologist for something." What are several everyday things that people become experts at defending passionately?

Even those who don't see themselves as apologists make a case for Christianity with their lives in some manner or another. When is a time that you represented your faith well by the way you lived? When was a time you failed to live out your beliefs?

What does Os Guinness mean when he writes, "We are in the grand secular age of apologetics"? Give a current example that validates this observation.

Do you agree that we live in a world where almost everyone is in "the business of relentless self-promotion"? In what situations are you most tempted to take part in this self-promotional frenzy? What have been the results when you have done so?

Guinness writes, "The great goals of life are to gain the widest possible public attention and to reach as many people in the world with our products—and always, our leading product is Us." If that is true, we are the biggest apologists for . . . ourselves. What are some ways you can break this cycle so you focus more on defending God's truth than yourself?

③ Christianity: A Historical Faith
Evidence That Demands a Verdict, page xxxvii

Christianity appeals to history. Specifically, it appeals to facts of history that can be examined through the normal means of historicity. As theologian Clark Pinnock stated, "The facts backing the Christian claim are not a special kind of religious fact. They are the cognitive, informational facts upon which all historical, legal, and ordinary decisions are based."[10] Luke, in the introduction to his Gospel, demonstrated this historical nature of Christianity:

> Inasmuch as many have taken in hand to set in order a narrative of those things which have been fulfilled among us, just as those who from the beginning were eyewitnesses and ministers of the word delivered them to us, it seemed good to me also, having had perfect understanding of all things from the very first, to write to you an orderly account, most excellent Theophilus, that you may know the certainty of those things in which you were instructed (1:1–4).

According to Luke, among these historical and knowable events was the resurrection of Jesus Christ, an event that was validated by Jesus himself through "many proofs" during a forty-day period and before numerous witnesses (see Acts 1:3). Make no mistake—the historical facts matter for Christianity. The Christian faith is an *objective* faith. Therefore, it must have an object that is *worthy* of faith. Salvation comes not from the *strength* of our beliefs but from the *object* of our beliefs. Yes, salvation comes through faith (see John 6:29; Ephesians 2:8–9), but the merit of faith depends on the object believed (not the faith *itself*).

One time, Josh debated the head of the philosophy department of a Midwestern university. In answering a question, he happened to mention the importance of the resurrection. At that point, his opponent interrupted and sarcastically said, "Come on, McDowell, the key issue is not whether the resurrection took place or not. The key issue is this: 'Do you believe it took place?'" He was hinting at—even boldly asserting—that Josh's *believing* was the most important thing.

Josh retorted, "Sir, it does matter whether the resurrection took place, because the value of Christian faith is not in the one believing, but in the One who is believed in, its object." He continued, "If anyone can demonstrate to me that Christ was not raised from the dead, I would not have a justifiable right to my Christian faith." As Christians, we must avoid the attitude, "Don't confuse me with the facts—my mind is made up!" The historical events reported in the Scriptures are essential. This is why Paul said, "If Christ is not risen, then our preaching is empty, and your faith is also empty" (1 Corinthians 15:14).

The world tends to minimize Christianity by saying it is just one of many religious faiths. How does it change things to say that Christianity is a *historical* faith?

Clark Pinnock wrote, "The facts backing the Christian claim are not a special kind of religious fact. They are the cognitive, informational facts upon which all historical, legal, and ordinary decisions are based." Does this give you a different perspective on pursuing evidence for Christianity? If so, how?

Read Acts 1:1–3. How does Luke show that he intended his Gospel and the book of Acts to be historically accurate? What evidence does Luke provide for this historical accuracy?

As noted earlier, Christians have to be careful to avoid the attitude, "Don't confuse me with the facts—my mind is made up!" Where in your faith do you most struggle with a tightly held belief . . . even if the facts do not support it? Explain.

What might it take for you to release that belief? Are you willing to ask God for the humility to go where the evidence leads on this issue? Why or why not?

❹ Christianity: A Testable Faith
Evidence That Demands a Verdict, page xxxviii

As Paul makes clear in his first letter to the Corinthians, Christianity is a historical religion tied to the life, teachings, death, and resurrection of Jesus. These claims are *testable*, in that anyone can actually examine their validity and determine historically whether they are reliable. As Paul noted, "If Christ is not risen, your faith is futile; you are still in your sins!" (1 Corinthians 15:17). Craig Hazen, a professor of apologetics, considers this to be one of the strangest passages in all of religious literature. He writes:

> I have not been able to find a passage in the Scriptures and teachings of the other great religious traditions that so tightly links the truth of an entire system of belief to a single, testable historical event. . . . This idea that the truth of Christianity is linked to the resurrection of Jesus in a testable way does set Christianity apart from the other great world religious traditions in a dramatic fashion. When you boil it down, Hinduism, Buddhism, and the like are about inner, personal experience and not about objective public knowledge. Other traditions *seem* to be about objective knowledge until you probe a little more deeply. Mormonism, for instance, seems to be about hidden gold plates, Jesus' ancient visit to the Western hemisphere, and latter-day prophets—things that could certainly, in principle, be evaluated in an objective way. However, when facing evidence contrary to these claims, the Mormon missionary, scholar, or apostle steps back and begins to talk about the special inner knowledge, a "burning in the bosom," that is the only confirmation that really counts about these unusual stories. At the end of the day, the Mormon is no different from the Buddhist in that they both rely on inner experience as their ultimate source and warrant for religious knowledge.[11]

Read 1 Corinthians 15:14–17. What does Paul say are the consequences for his preaching if Christ is not risen?

What does Paul say are the consequences for believers everywhere if Christ did not rise from the dead?

Why do you think Craig Hazen considers this to be one of the strangest passages in all of religious literature? Explain your answer.

What does Hazen say sets Christianity apart from the other great world religious traditions—like Hinduism and Buddhism—in dramatic fashion?

Prior to this week's teaching, did you view Christianity as a "testable faith"? How does this session shift your view of Christianity in comparison to other religions?

❺ Being a Relational Apologist
Evidence That Demands a Verdict, page lvi

Believers often want to know what is the "silver bullet" argument that proves Christianity. But the truth is that *there is no argument you can make that can force anyone to believe.* Given this, how should Christians engage their neighbors? We suggest four ways.

First, be *gentle and humble*. As discussed in this week's teaching, Jesus reasoned with the religious leaders of his day, providing multiple lines of evidence that he was the Son of God. And yet, though he was divine, he willingly humbled himself for the sake of loving others (see Philippians 2:5–7). We can do no less. As Philosopher Dallas Willard observed, "Like Jesus, we are reaching out in love in a humble spirit with no coercion. The only way to accomplish that is to present our defense gently, as help offered in love in the manner of Jesus."[12]

Second, be *relational*. While labels can sometimes be helpful, depersonalizing people by putting them into various boxes can cause harm. If labels cause you to ignore the unique personhood of *every* individual, you need to reexamine how you are using them. It is critical to have genuine relationships with people who are atheists, agnostics, and others who hold a variety of worldviews. Your goal is not simply to *convert* them but to *value* them as human beings. Apologetics is an explanation you offer to help people you deeply care about.

Third, be *studious*. Know what you are talking about and do thorough research to back up your claims. Critically examine your arguments and understand both sides of every issue. Study both sides and talk about your findings with fellow Christians and non-Christians. Do the hard work of learning a discipline and presenting the truth fairly and accurately.

Finally, be a *practitioner*. Young people today prize authenticity. They want to know not only if you can make a good argument but also whether your life reflects the truth you proclaim. If your life doesn't reflect your truth claims, what you say will fall on deaf ears. If you claim to believe in the deity of Jesus, is he really Lord in your life? If you believe in the resurrection, does it shape how you face death? How does your belief in the truth of the Bible really shape how you treat people? Actively live the truth you proclaim.

Do you wish there was a "silver bullet" argument to prove Christianity? Why do you think that God did not choose to provide us with one?

What are the four essential characteristics for an apologist who wants to engage others? Which of those four is the most challenging for you? Why?

As an apologist, it is easy to forget that your ultimate purpose is to value other persons as you share about God and truth. This is far more important than convincing them you are right. How can you nurture genuine relationships with those you engage?

A relational apologist must invest a generous amount of time to understand both sides of an issue in order to reach the person who sees the issue differently. Do you find that difficult to do? If so, why? If not, give an example of how you have done this.

In the end, it all comes down to whether our lives reflect the truth we proclaim. Let's not allow pride, guilt, or shame to overcome us. The goal isn't perfection, but a lifelong commitment to loving God and loving others with all our heart, mind, soul, and strength. Given that, how are you doing in living what you believe?

Recommended Reading

Use the space below to write any key insights or questions from your personal study that you want to discuss at the next group meeting. In preparation for that meeting, you may wish to review chapters 1 and 27–28 in *Evidence That Demands a Verdict*.

IS THERE SUCH A THING AS TRUTH?

Jesus answered, "You say rightly that I am a king.
For this cause I was born, and for this cause I have come into the world,
that I should bear witness to the truth. Everyone who is of the truth
hears My voice." Pilate said to Him, "What is truth?"

JOHN 18:37–38

Welcome

The study of truth might seem irrelevant to our daily lives—a topic that is perhaps better reserved for the ivory-tower academic types. In our everyday world, defining truth rarely ranks high on our list of priorities. We may even ask, "Why do we need to worry about truth anyway?"

The reality is that this is one of the *most* important questions we can ask. Today, we live in what is known as a post-truth society. This is tragic, because there really is no pursuit more worthy than understanding and following the truth . . . wherever it may lead. In fact, even though we may not think about truth a lot, our actions reveal how much we value it. For instance, when we type an address in on our phone, we want the *true* directions to get there. When our boss schedules a meeting, we want the true time when we should be there. When we visit the doctor, we want the *true* test results, not something made up.

We innately know that to live a life in truth is better than to be fooled or to fool ourselves. Truth is a worthy goal for its own sake, and we seek it because we intuitively know that it is valuable. As Stewart E. Kelly, a professor of philosophy, writes:

> Convenient fictions are nevertheless fictions, and most people want more than that. This point is nicely illustrated in the popular movie *The Matrix*. Here the main character is given a set of choices, each involving a particular pill. Pill 1 will give him a life of perfect illusion. He will not even remember that he ever chose such a pill. But if he chooses pill 2, then he will find out about both his life and reality, "a truth he is warned will be unpleasant. He chooses, unsurprisingly to the audience, the truth." Pill 2 is the better option because, in part, humans are truth seekers. But another key reason is that knowing the truth is *ceteris paribus*, an intrinsically good state of affairs.[1]

In this second session, we are going to look at the big questions surrounding the topic of truth. We will examine *what truth is*, *why it is important*, *how we can know it*, and what is the *evidence for its existence*. Far from an academic study, you will find that the answers will affect every aspect of your daily life in both personal and practical ways.[2]

Share

If you or any of your group members are just getting to know one another, take a few minutes to introduce yourselves. Next, begin by discussing one of the following questions:

- Popular culture and political groups are adamant that we need to be more open-minded and should not judge one other's moral values. Do you agree with this stance? Why or why not?

or —

- We live in a post-truth society that believes feelings trump truth. What would you say if someone asked you, "Why is truth even important? Isn't how I sincerely feel about an issue what matters most?"

Read

Invite someone to read aloud the following passage from John 8:27–36. Listen for fresh insight and then share any new thoughts with the group using the questions that follow.

Then they said to Him, "Who are You?"
And Jesus said to them, "Just what I have been saying to you from the beginning. I have many things to say and to judge

concerning you, but He who sent Me is true; and I speak to the world those things which I heard from Him."

They did not understand that He spoke to them of the Father.

Then Jesus said to them, "When you lift up the Son of Man, then you will know that I am He, and that I do nothing of Myself; but as My Father taught Me, I speak these things. And He who sent Me is with Me. The Father has not left Me alone, for I always do those things that please Him." As He spoke these words, many believed in Him.

Then Jesus said to those Jews who believed Him, "If you abide in My word, you are My disciples indeed. And you shall know the truth, and the truth shall make you free."

They answered Him, "We are Abraham's descendants, and have never been in bondage to anyone. How can You say, 'You will be made free'?"

Jesus answered them, "Most assuredly, I say to you, whoever commits sin is a slave of sin. And a slave does not abide in the house forever, but a son abides forever. Therefore if the Son makes you free, you shall be free indeed."

What does Jesus believe about our ability to know truth?

Why does the truth make us free? Without truth, to what do we remain enslaved?

The crowd around Jesus was offended by the inference they were not already free. What parallels do you see in today's society regarding the attitude that says we are all free to pursue whatever we think is right? Explain.

Watch

Play the video for session two. As you watch, use the following outline to record any thoughts or concepts that stand out to you.

Notes

Twenty-five years ago, few questioned the existence of *objective* truth (what can be observed). Then truth became *subjective* (what you think). Now truth is *emotional* (what you feel).

The dictionary defines *truth* as "that which has fidelity to the original." In other words, for something to be true, it must be the same or equal to the original.

The Correspondence Theory of Truth states that if a belief or an idea corresponds to reality, it is true. If not, then it must be false.

Many people accept there is truth in the little things (like weather forecasts or disciplines like math or science) but disown the concept of truth when it comes to morality or religion. The claims of

Christianity happened in a historical setting. The claims are either true … or false.

It's often said all religions lead to God, but if you look at the wildly different and exclusive claims of each, they fundamentally contradict the other claims. It is possible for them to all be false, but it is impossible for them to all be true.

It makes sense to start our search for truth with Jesus Christ, because he was the primary religious leader who claimed to be God.

. . . .

TRUTH IS THE MOST IMPORTANT PURSUIT

In the childhood years, wonder can be attained by dabbling in the world of fantasy. That is both the glory and the fragility of childhood. But as the years pass, wonder is eroded in the face of reality and in the recognition that life may not be lived in a fairy-tale world. A displacement is brought about by the ever-increasing demand of the mind, not just for the fantastic, but for the true. The search for truth then becomes all-pervasive, encompassing implications for the essence and destiny of life itself. Even if not overtly admitted, the search for truth is nevertheless hauntingly present, propelled by the need for incontrovertible answers to four inescapable questions, those dealing with origin, meaning, morality, and destiny. No thinking person can avoid this search, and it can only end when one is convinced that the answers espoused are truth. Aristotle was right when he opined that all philosophy begins with wonder; but the journey, I suggest, can only progress through truth.[3]

— RAVI ZACHARIAS

. . . .

Discuss

Take a few minutes with your group members to discuss what you just watched and explore these concepts in Scripture.

1. In your own words, how would you define *truth*?

2. Our culture has transitioned from seeing truth as objective data to defining it as whatever an individual embraces (or feels) it is. What is problematic about this shifting view of truth?

3. During the teaching, Josh used an example of a liter of water to represent the concept of fidelity. What does this demonstrate? How does this illustration help you to understand the concept of truth?

4. In what ways do those who say truth isn't important contradict themselves by their daily reliance on truth? What might their actions reveal about their beliefs on a deeper level?

5. Jesus' statements in the Bible are claims that can be proven, by the evidence, as either true or false. Have you considered that your faith and beliefs are evidence-based? How does knowing this increase your confidence when discussing the issue of truth with others?

6. What is the "ad hominem fallacy?" What is the weakness of this approach?

Respond

As philosopher Douglas Groothuis writes, "The Bible does not present truth as a cultural creation of the ancient Jews or the early Christians. They received truth from the God who speaks truth to his creatures, and they were expected by this God to conform themselves to this truth."[4] Jesus claims to be *the* truth. This claim has huge implications for our study on truth, since it suggests that it is impossible to know truth fully apart from a relationship with Jesus as Savior and Lord. Today, close out your time by selecting two passages from the list below related to biblical truth, and then write down the implications this has for your life.

Verse(s)	The Implications for Your Life
John 8:31–32: "If you abide in My word, you are My disciples indeed. And you shall know the truth, and the truth shall make you free."	

Verse(s)	The Implications for Your Life
John 14:6: "I am the way, the truth, and the life. No one comes to the Father except through Me."	
John 16:13: "However, when He, the Spirit of truth, has come, He will guide you into all truth; for He will not speak on His own authority, but whatever He hears He will speak; and He will tell you things to come."	
Ephesians 1:13: "In Him you also trusted, after you heard the word of truth, the gospel of your salvation; in whom also, having believed, you were sealed with the Holy Spirit of promise."	
1 Corinthians 13:4, 6: "Love suffers long and is kind . . . does not rejoice in iniquity, but rejoices in the truth."	
2 Timothy 2:15: "Be diligent to present yourself approved to God, a worker who does not need to be ashamed, rightly dividing the word of truth."	
1 John 1:8: "If we say that we have no sin, we deceive ourselves, and the truth is not in us."	

Verse(s)	The Implications for Your Life
1 John 4:6: "We are of God. He who knows God hears us; he who is not of God does not hear us. By this we know the spirit of truth and the spirit of error."	

Pray

Wrap up your time by taking a few moments to pray together. Here are a few ideas of what you could pray about based on the topics of this session:

- Express your thankfulness that you live in a world where truth can be known.
- Ask Jesus to reveal how his claims to be God are based in absolute truth.
- Pray that you will be grounded in truth rather than what "feels right."
- Invite God to give you a humble and teachable spirit in your search for truth.

BETWEEN-SESSIONS
PERSONAL STUDY

Reflect on the material you've covered this week by engaging in any or all of the following between-sessions activities. Each day offers a short reading from *Evidence That Demands a Verdict*, along with a few reflection questions to take you deeper into the theme of this week's study. Journal or write down your thoughts after each question. At the start of the next session, you will have a few minutes to share any insights you learned.

❶ The Uniqueness of the Bible
Evidence That Demands a Verdict, page 3

You will often hear people say, "You don't read the Bible, do you?" Or they will remark, "The Bible is just another book. You really ought to read—" and then they will name some of their favorite books. Others who have a Bible in their library describe how it sits on the shelf next to other "greats" such as Homer's *Odyssey*, Shakespeare's *Romeo and Juliet*, or Austen's *Pride and Prejudice*. Their Bible may be dusty, but they still recognize its historical influence.

Still others make degrading comments about the Bible because they are surprised anyone might take it seriously enough to spend time reading it. I (Josh) was once like them. I tried to refute the Bible as God's Word to humanity. I finally concluded, however, that *not* accepting the Bible must result from being either biased, prejudiced, or simply unread. As I continued to study the Bible, I concluded the best word to describe it is *unique.*

In particular, I have found there are three essential teachings that distinguish the Bible from all other religious and secular worldviews. These teachings include (1) the Trinity, (2) the incarnation and atonement, and (3) faith versus works. Without all three, one would no longer be speaking of biblical Christianity—and one would not know the truth.

Rooted deeply in the pages of Scripture is the understanding of the *Trinity*, or the view that God is one divine nature (essence) existing in three eternal persons—the Father, Son, and Holy Spirit. How is God's essential oneness expressed in the following verses?

Deuteronomy 6:4

1 Corinthians 8:6

How do the following passages support the divinity of each person within the Trinity?

2 Corinthians 1:2 (*the Father*)

John 1:1, 14 (*the Son*)

1 Corinthians 2:10–11 (*the Holy Spirit*)

The Bible reveals Jesus was fully God but also fully human. This is known as the *incarnation*—God *becoming* human. What do the following verses reveal about Jesus' humanity?

Luke 2:7 (*Jesus' birth*)

Matthew 26:37 (*Jesus' emotions*)

John 4:6 (*Jesus' physical limitations*)

The final reconciliation of humans to their Creator was accomplished through what is known as the *atonement*—which can be defined as "the work Christ did in his life and death to earn our salvation."[5] What do the following verses state about the atonement?

Romans 3:23–25

Galatians 3:13

1 John 2:2

Christianity alone proclaims that God offers all people the salvation they absolutely cannot achieve on their own. Write Ephesians 2:8–9 below in whatever Bible translation you typically use. What is your takeaway from this passage?

The Bible also affirms a person's value is found in his or her being, not in that person's behavior. How do the following verses explain that your inherent worth are based on how you were created?

Genesis 1:27

Genesis 9:6

❷ Subjective and Objective Truth
Evidence That Demands a Verdict, page 612

Statements about "truth" that change from person to person, or are based on circumstances, are known as subjective claims. These primarily have to do with a personal preferences or desires. The reason they are called *subjective* is because the beliefs of the *subject* are the determining factor as to whether the claims are deemed true or not. In other words, if the subject believes something, then it is true for him or her.

In my (Sean's) book *Ethix,* I write, "Knowing truth helps us to make right moral decisions. But not all decisions in life deal with morality. Most choices we make, in fact, are not moral choices at all. *Should we go bowling tonight, or should we go to the movies? Do*

I prefer Chocolate-Peanut-Butter-Cup or Cookies-and-Cream ice cream? Should I wear my green shirt or my black shirt? These are personal choices relative to the individual. The way one would answer these questions would be considered subjective truths. The phrase 'Chocolate ice cream is the best flavor' may be true for you but not for me. These types of truths are based on preference or feeling and can easily change."[6]

Subjective claims apply to a person's preferences. However, *objective* truth deals with the real world that is independent from our perception of it. Objective truths are true no matter what a person prefers or happens to believe. They do not change because of one's thoughts or whims. They depend on the *object* itself. As I write, "Objective truths . . . are based on the external world. They are related to the world independently of how we think or feel. For example, the sentences '1 + 2 = 3,' 'George Washington was the first president of the United States,' and 'Sacramento is the capital of California,' are all objective truths; that is, they are accurate statements even if we don't believe them."[7]

How would you define subjective truth?

Give an example of subjective truth in your life. In subjective truth, who is the subject?

How would you define objective truth? How does it differ from subjective truth?

Truth can be defined as correspondence to reality. Does that mean truth is subjective or objective? What if we disagree with—or don't prefer—what is true?

Why do you think that there is so much confusion today regarding truth?

❸ Everything Is *Not* Relative
Evidence That Demands a Verdict, pages 613–614

Those who argue that all truth is subjective espouse a form of *relativism*. Relativism creeps into our vocabulary in statements such as, "Well, that's true for you, but not for me." Unfortunately, those who hold to relativism have to deal with a number of problems. Let's consider just two of the main ones.

First, *relativism is self-defeating*. Relativists put themselves between a rock and a hard place with their stance. Either they have to deny objective truth fully (and even their own position) for the sake of consistency, or they have to embrace that which they are denying. As philosopher Paul Copan explains, "To be consistent, the relativist must say, 'Nothing is objectively true—including my own position. So you're free to accept my view or reject it.'"[8] The self-defeating nature of relativism soon becomes clear: the very nature of the claim contradicts the claims itself. One cannot hold to relativism and insist others do so as well.

Second, *relativism leads to absurd logical outcomes*. The logical outcomes that naturally flow from the relativists' viewpoint leaves no room for morality, ethics, human value, or common sense. In fact, relativism undermines even the value of humanity. As Christian apologist Gregory Koukl explains, "The death of truth in our society has created a moral decay in which 'every debate ends with the barroom question "says who?"' When we abandon the idea that one set of laws applies to every human being, all that remains is subjective, personal opinion. . . . If there is no truth, nothing has transcendent value, including human beings."[9]

Relativism sounds like a relaxed approach to life. How can something so easygoing create so many unexpected problems?

In what ways is relativism self-defeating?

How can relativism lead to such a logically absurd outcome?

On a more serious level, how can relativism undermine the value of humanity?

If you met with a committed relativist, how might you kindly—but convincingly—articulate the fatal flaws in that person's stance?

❹ The Biblical View of Truth
Evidence That Demands a Verdict, pages 608, 618

The *correspondence theory of truth* has been around for a long time (since the days of the Greek philosophers such as Plato and Aristotle) and has withstood many challenges. It is, by far, the most believed theory about the nature of truth, for it states that truth is that which corresponds to its referent (that to which it refers). As philosopher and apologist J. P. Moreland summarizes, "In its simplest form, the correspondence theory of truth is the view that a claim—technically, a proposition—is true just in case it corresponds to reality; that is, a proposition is true when what it asserts to be the case is the case."[10]

In recent years, some scholars have taken to defending the biblical idea of truth. They discovered that although the Bible does not explicitly articulate the correspondence theory of truth, it implicitly assumes the correspondence principle throughout its pages. One example is found in the way the Old Testament applied the test of correspondence in determining whether a prophet truly spoke from God: "When a prophet speaks in the name of the LORD, if the thing does not happen or come to pass, that is the thing which the LORD has not spoken; the prophet has spoken it presumptuously (Deuteronomy 18:22). The test of correspondence settles the question.

Another example is found in the New Testament, when the Pharisees and lawyers challenged Jesus for telling a man that his sins were forgiven. Jesus' response employed a double use of the correspondence theory. He invited them to reason about which was easier: to declare something that is invisible or something that was visible. Then, prefacing his action, he told the Pharisees why he was undertaking it: so "that you may know that the Son of Man has power on earth to forgive sins." Then he directed the paralyzed man to "arise, take up your bed, and go to your house" (Luke 5:24).

The correspondence between hearing Jesus' words and seeing the man walk was a test of the truth of what Jesus said.

How would you define the correspondence theory of truth in your own words?

Why do you think this is the most believed theory about the nature of truth?

How does the Bible employ the correspondence theory of truth?

When the Pharisees and lawyers confronted Jesus for forgiving a man's sins, how did Jesus' response reflect a double use of the correspondence theory?

Read Romans 1:18. How does this reflect the biblical idea of truth?

The Knowability of Truth
Evidence That Demands a Verdict, pages 621–623

We can *know* truth. If that statement sounds bold, arrogant, or outrageous, it is primarily because we live in a world that is *skeptical* of truth. The field of philosophy that deals with how we know things is called *epistemology*. Essentially, it is the study of knowledge.

One of the most important debates in epistemology today is known as "the problem of the criterion." The issue involves what we know and how we know it. In other words: *What do we know, and what is our criterion for knowledge?* There are three primary ways that philosophers seek to resolve these questions. The first response is *skepticism*. The skeptic simply questions or denies that we have knowledge.

The second response is called *methodism*. This view holds that we must first have a criterion before we can evaluate any claim about knowledge. In other words, we begin with a criterion and then find claims that meet the chosen criterion. The problem with this approach, however, is that it leads to an infinite regress. This is because if each knowledge claim requires a criterion, that criterion would need a further criterion—and so on, ad infinitum.

The third response is called *particularism*. As J. P. Moreland explains, "According to particularists, we start by knowing specific, clear items of knowledge: for example, that I had eggs for breakfast this morning . . . that $7 + 5 = 12$, that mercy is a virtue, and so on. I can know some things directly and simply without needing criteria for how I know them and without having to know how or even that I know them. We know many things without being able to prove that we do or without fully understanding them."[11]

How does this work in practice? Moreland notes, "I may start with moral knowledge (murder is wrong) and legal knowledge (taxes are to be paid by April 15) and go on to formulate criteria for when something is moral or legal. I could then use these criteria for judging borderline cases (intentionally driving on the wrong side of the street, for example). In general, we start with clear instances of knowledge, formulate criteria based on those clear instances, and extend our knowledge by using those criteria in borderline, unclear cases."[12]

In other words, we all operate by assuming we have knowledge in *some* realms. Even skeptics who claim we cannot have knowledge assume that they know we cannot have knowledge. Believing we really *do* have knowledge is thus the inevitable conclusion.

What two issues does "the problem of the criterion" address? Why is it so important for Christians to be familiar with this topic?

What are the three primary ways for people to address the questions about what they know?

How would you define skepticism and methodism? What are the Achilles' heels of these claims?

What is particularism? How does this approach allow you to start with something you know and then extend that knowledge to a less defined issue?

What is an example of something you do on a daily basis based on the assumption that certain truths are knowable? Why do you think it is difficult for some people to accept that people can—and, in fact, do—know truth?

Recommended Reading

Use the space below to write any key insights or questions from your personal study that you want to discuss at the next group meeting. In preparation for that meeting, you may wish to review chapters 2–3 and 6 in *Evidence That Demands a Verdict*.

SESSION THREE

IS THE NEW TESTAMENT RELIABLE?

The word of God is living and powerful, and sharper than any
two-edged sword, piercing even to the division of soul and spirit,
and of joints and marrow, and is a discerner of the thoughts
and intents of the heart. And there is no creature hidden from
His sight, but all things are naked and open to the eyes of Him
to whom we must give account.

HEBREWS 4:12–13

Welcome

A common objection that critics of the Bible raise is that the New Testament is not historically reliable—that the stories of Jesus' miracles and resurrection developed over time and are thus far more legend than they are fact. Noted scholar Bart D. Ehrman summed up this position in an interview when he stated, "My view is that the earliest followers of Jesus had an exaltation Christology. They knew Jesus as a man, but they came to believe he had been raised from the dead. Once they thought that, they assumed he had been taken up to heaven and made divine. As time went on, other Christians began to think that Jesus was not originally a human, but that he was a divine being for his entire life, and then an incarnation theology developed."[1]

The historical reliability of the New Testament is an important topic for all believers today—and it should be tested by the same criteria through which all historical documents are tested. But for believers in Christ, the topic is even more important because the majority of what we know about its central character—Jesus—comes from the information we find in the New Testament. It is critical that we can know with certainty that he was an *actual* person who lived in an *actual* place at an *actual* time in history and *actually* did the things reported of him.

This is where a science known as *historiography* comes into play. Historiography is a big word but simply represents the process and the principles by which scholars can determine the authenticity of any document—whether it be from Plato, Plutarch, Herodotus, or anyone else. In applying this science, scholars put ancient documents through three specific tests.

The first is known as the *internal evidence test*, which examines whether one can trust the writings internally by looking at the document. The second is the *bibliographical test*, which focuses on how many manuscripts there are and how close they are to the original document (known as the *autograph*). The third is the *external evidence test,* which examines whether there is any external evidence outside of the book to support its claims.

In this third session, we will apply these same tests to the New Testament to determine whether we are standing on firm ground when we assert that it is, in fact, historically reliable.[2]

Share

Begin your group time by inviting anyone to share his or her insights from last week's personal study. Next, discuss one of the following questions:

- What event in the New Testament do you think people outside the church have the most difficult time believing? What is the hardest for *you* to believe?

— or —

- What tests do you apply to a claim to determine whether it is true? Why is it important to subject the New Testament to this type of scrutiny?

Read

Invite someone to read aloud the following passage from Acts 4:13–20. Listen for fresh insight and then share any new thoughts with the group using the questions that follow.

Now when [the Jewish religious leaders] saw the boldness of Peter and John, and perceived that they were uneducated and untrained men, they marveled. And they realized that they had been with Jesus. And seeing the man who had been healed standing with them, they could say nothing against it. But when they had commanded them to go aside out of the council, they conferred among themselves, saying, "What shall we do to these men? For, indeed, that a notable miracle has been done through them is evident to all who dwell in Jerusalem, and we cannot deny it. But so that it spreads no further among the people, let us severely threaten them, that from now on they speak to no man in this name."

So they called them and commanded them not to speak at all nor teach in the name of Jesus. But Peter and John answered and said to them, "Whether it is right in the sight of God to listen to you more than to God, you judge. For we cannot but speak the things which we have seen and heard."

How does picturing this scene as an actual historical event change your perspective of it?

Notice how the Jewish religious leaders responded to the miracle that Peter and John had performed. They admitted they had weighed the evidence (the healing of a man) and found it to be true. What did they decide to do with this truthful evidence? What was their motivation?

Peter and John—in the face of great physical peril—refused to remain silent. Does their determination to speak the truth at any cost give you confidence in the reliability of their eyewitness testimony? Why or why not?

Watch

Play the video for session three. As you watch, use the following outline to record any thoughts or concepts that stand out to you.

Notes

A foundational question for any Christian today is whether we can trust the New Testament to be accurate and reliable.

Historiography helps us determine the authenticity of an ancient document by using three primary tests: (1) the internal evidence test, (2) the bibliography test, and (3) the external evidence test.

The *internal evidence test* examines whether a document is coherent, consistent, cohesive, and confirming. Can the writing be trusted? Does it have the ring of authenticity? Does the author claim to be reporting truth or just writing a piece of fiction?

- The writers of the New Testament claimed to be writing the truth, and they backed it up with eyewitness testimony that could be verified.

- It is also clear the writers of the New Testament care most about truth because they are willing to report embarrassing material—even if it disparages their own reputation.

The *bibliographical test* examines questions related to the manuscripts and documents. How many hand-written copies exist? How many discrepancies are there? What is the distance from the original document (the autograph) to the closest copy?

- Textual critics like to point out the number of variances in copies of the New Testament, but in reality those are overstated—and most relate just spelling errors.

- For most ancient documents, the closest copy to the original is at least 300 to 400 years. For the New Testament, it is, at most, only fifty years from the original.

The *external evidence test* examines what external evidence exists outside of the manuscript (such as historical reports and archaeology) that support the claims within the document.

- Historians such as Tacitus, Suetonius, and Josephus mention Jesus in their works and relate the basic timeline of Jesus found in the New Testament.

- There are also countless findings from archaeology that consistently confirm the writers of the New Testament got it correct.

Based on these three tests, you can stand on firm ground and with confidence say, "Thus saith the Lord." This is what Josh concluded as a non-believer.

. . . .

THE CONNECTION BETWEEN CHRISTIANITY AND HISTORICAL EVENTS

True Christianity, the Christianity of the New Testament documents, is absolutely dependent on history [including its manuscript attestation]. At the heart of the New Testament faith is the assertion that "God was in Christ reconciling the world to Himself" (2 Corinthians 5:19). The incarnation, death, and resurrection of Jesus Christ as a real event in time and space, i.e., as historical realities, are the indispensable foundations of the Christian faith. To my mind, then, Christianity is best defined as the recitation of, the celebration of, and the participation in God's acts in history, which as the New Testament writing emphasize have found their culmination in Jesus Christ.[3]

DONALD HAGNER

. . . .

Discuss

Take a few minutes with your group members to discuss what you just watched and explore these concepts in Scripture.

1. What is *historiography*? Why is it essential to understanding the New Testament?

2. Do you believe there is a significant difference between investigating whether the Bible is the inspired word of God and researching whether it is reliable and true from a historical point of view? Explain.

3. With the New Testament being the document under investigation, what would be an example of an *internal evidence test*? A *bibliographical test*? An *external evidence test*?

4. The members of the early church were very interested in the eyewitness accounts reported in the New Testament, as they were staking their lives on whether that testimony was true. How does this lend support to the claim that the New Testament is historically accurate?

5. Today, there are some 27,000 ancient copies of the New Testament in existence. Why is this abundance of copies so important when it comes to determining the text of the original? How does this help us to know the historical accuracy of the original was preserved?

6. After applying the three tests, the findings reveal there is greater evidence for the historical accuracy of the New Testament than

most other literature in antiquity. How does this affect your confidence in trusting the claims made in the New Testament?

Respond

When police officers are investigating a crime, they will look not only to the testimony of eyewitnesses but also to whether those testimonies agree with one another. Investigators will rely on this type of agreement, known as *corroborating evidence*, to determine the facts of the case and decide how to best move forward. When it comes to the New Testament, the same type of method can be applied. Today, close out your time by reviewing two passages listed below that relate to certain individuals who saw Jesus alive after his crucifixion. Write the name of the person(s) and then write a brief summary of what each person witnessed.

Passage	Person(s)	What the Person(s) Witnessed
Matthew 28:1–10		
Luke 24:13–27		
John 20:19–2		

Passage	Person(s)	What the Person(s) Witnessed
John 20:25–29		
Acts 9:1–5		
1 Corinthians 15:6		
1 Corinthians 15:7		

Pray

Wrap up your time by taking a few moments to pray together. Here are a few ideas of what you could pray about based on the topics of this session:

- Express your thankfulness that the New Testament is reliable and true.
- Thank God that the New Testament holds up to scrutiny when examined.
- Ask God to give you a hunger for understanding the Bible.
- Ask God to help those with doubts about the Bible's accuracy.
- Pray that more archaeological discoveries will be made that verify Scripture.

Reflect on the material you've covered this week by engaging in any or all of the following between-sessions activities. Each day offers a short reading from *Evidence That Demands a Verdict*, along with a few reflection questions to take you deeper into the theme of this week's study. Journal or write down your thoughts after each question. At the start of the next session, you will have a few minutes to share any insights you learned.

❶ Who Decided What to Include in the Bible?
Evidence That Demands a Verdict, pages 25–26

The New Testament is divided into twenty-seven "books." But just *how* were these books—and not others—chosen to be part of the New Testament? The question relates to *canonicity*. The third-century church father Origen used the word *canon* "to denote what we call the 'rule of faith,' the standard by which we are to measure and evaluate everything that may be offered to us as an article of belief."[4] Later, the term meant a "list" or "index."[5] As applied to Scripture, the word *canon* means "an officially accepted list of books."[6]

According to scholar Michael Kruger, there were three primary beliefs held by Christians in the early church that led to the formation of the New Testament. First, *Christians in the early church believed the Old Testament was unfinished.* "The fact that Second Temple Jews [those living 515 BC–AD 70] regarded the Old Testament story as incomplete and in need of a proper conclusion has significant implications for the production of a new corpus of biblical books. If some Second Temple Jews became convinced that the story was completed in the life and ministry of Jesus of Nazareth—such as the earliest Christians did—then it is not unreasonable to think that the proper conclusion to the Old Testament might then be written."[7]

Second, *Christians in the early church believed God was ushering in a new covenant.* If the Old Testament was seen as the written form of the Mosaic Covenant, then the Christians of the early church would sense the need for a written form of the fulfillment of the New Covenant (mentioned in Jeremiah 31:31–34). "The covenantal context of early Christianity suggests that the emergence of a new corpus of scriptural books, after the announcement of a new covenant, could not be regarded as entirely unexpected."[8]

Third, *Christians of the early church believed the apostles possessed the authority of Christ.* "If apostles were viewed as the mouthpiece of Christ, and it was believed that they wrote down that apostolic message in books, then those books would be received as the very words of Christ himself. . . . For this reason, a written New Testament was not something the church formally 'decided' to have at some later date, but was instead the natural outworking of the early church's view of the function of the apostles."[9]

How did the church father Origen define the word *canon*?

What does the term *canon* mean when applied to Scripture?

Christians in the early church viewed Jesus as not just a prophet but as the fulfillment of the Old Testament prophecies concerning the Messiah. How did their ability to see their faith as an ongoing story help pave the way for the formation of the New Testament?

Read Jeremiah 31:31–34. How was this prophecy pivotal in the early church's understanding of why a "New" Testament was needed?

How did the early Christians' view of the apostles pave the way for them to embracing their letters and other writings as part of a New Testament canon?

❷ The Internal Evidence Test

Evidence That Demands a Verdict, pages 69–70, 74–75

There are several ways that scholars apply the internal evidence test when checking whether an ancient document (like the New Testament) can be deemed historically accurate. Generally, this begins by giving the document *the benefit of the doubt* and not bringing any pre-supposed claims on the part of the researcher into the analysis. As noted scholar John Warwick Montgomery states, literary critics still follow Aristotle's dictum that "the benefit of the doubt is to be given to the document itself, not arrogated by the critic to himself . . . [therefore] one must listen to the claims of the document under analysis, and not assume fraud or error unless the author disqualified himself by contradictions or known factual inaccuracies."[10]

In addition, researchers attempt to determine whether the document is *free of known contradictions*. In the case of the New Testament, some Christians are troubled to find statements in one place that appear to contradict statements in other places. However, these apparent contradictions can be resolved with a little research. For example, the books of Matthew and Acts seem to give conflicting versions about the death of Judas Iscariot. Matthew relates Judas died by hanging himself (see 27:5). But in Acts, Luke reports that Judas fell headlong in a field, and "he burst open in the middle and all his entrails gushed out" (1:18).

It is perplexing as to how both accounts could be true. However, one can theorize that Judas hanged himself off the side of a cliff, the rope gave way, and then he fell headlong into the field below. It would be the only way a fall into a field could burst open a body. Sure enough, when you visit the traditional site of Judas's death in the Holy Land, you find a field at the bottom of a cliff outside the city of Jerusalem.

It is also important, when applying the internal evidence test, to determine *when the document was actually written*. In the case of the New Testament, the books were not written down a century or more after the events they described but during the lifetimes of those involved in the accounts. Therefore, the New Testament should be regarded as a competent primary source document from the first century.[11] It's interesting that among the Jews of this period, there were a small number of popular names and a large number of rare ones that are captured in the New Testament. As scholar Richard Bauckham notes: "It becomes very unlikely that the names in the Gospels are late accretions to the traditions. Outside Palestine the appropriate names simply could not have been chosen."[12]

What is Aristotle's dictum? Does it give higher priority to the document or the critic?

Why is it important, when applying the internal evidence test, to not approach the text with any pre-conceived assumptions or biases?

Read Matthew 27:3–8 and Acts 1:15–19. What similarities do you see in the accounts of Judas's death? What differences do you find?

Many scholars regard the New Testament as a competent primary source document from the first century. Why do they take this stance? Do you agree?

How does knowing the New Testament employs the same names that were prevalent during first-century Palestine strengthen the case for when it was written?

③ The Bibliographical Test
Evidence That Demands a Verdict, pages 46–47, 53, 61–63

The bibliographical test is an examination of the transmission by which copies of ancient documents have come to us today. In other words, because we do not have the original documents, we need to assess the reliability of the copies we do have by (1) determining the number of copies in existence, and (2) determining the time interval between the original copy and the currently existing copies.[13] For any ancient work, the greater the number of copies, and the earlier the dating of those manuscripts, the easier it is for us to reconstruct a text closer to the original and identify errors in subsequent copies.

When it comes to the New Testament, as with other documents of ancient literature, there are no known original manuscripts in existence. However, the abundance of copies of the New Testament makes it possible for us to reconstruct the original text with virtually complete accuracy.[14] We have more than 2.6 million pages of just the 5,800-plus Greek New Testament manuscripts. A stack of extant manuscripts for the average classical writer would measure about four feet high—which simply cannot compare to the more than one mile of New Testament manuscripts in existence today.[15]

The earliest verified New Testament Greek manuscript is the John Rylands Papyrus of John, known by the designation "P52," which scholar Bart Ehrman dates to AD 125–130, plus or minus twenty-five years. The Diatessaron, an early harmony of the Gospels, can be dated to c. AD 170. The earliest complete manuscripts of the entire New Testament, the Codex Vaticanus and Codex Sinaiticus, can be dated c. 325–350.

All told, the sheer number and earliness of the existing New Testament manuscripts give us great reason to believe the New Testament accurately transmits the content of the originals. In addition, as scholars Bruce Metzger and Bart Ehrman note, "Besides textual evidence derived from New Testament Greek manuscripts and from early versions, the textual critic has available the numerous scriptural quotations included in the commentaries, sermons, and other treatises written by the early Church fathers. Indeed, so extensive are these citations that if all other sources for our knowledge of the text of the New Testament were destroyed, they would be sufficient alone for the reconstruction of practically the entire New Testament."[16]

What are the two components involved in the bibliographical test?

How does having a large number of copies of a manuscript enable us to more accurately determine the content of the original?

Why is it important for the copies of that manuscript to be as close in time to the production of the original manuscript as possible?

Why is it significant that the early church fathers quoted widely from the books that make up the New Testament?"

The works that make up the New Testament were by far the most frequently copied and widely circulated books in antiquity. How does this one fact alone make you feel about its reliability?

④ The External Evidence Test
Evidence That Demands a Verdict, pages 78–79, 82

One of the key external evidence tests that scholars use to evaluate the accuracy of the New Testament is known as the *intention test.* This test evaluates whether an author from antiquity wrote his story with the intention of it being treated as historical fact. For instance, nobody treats "The Boy who Cried Wolf" story as historical, because it fails the intention test. It was written for a lesson . . . not for historical purposes.

When it comes to the stories in the Gospels about Jesus, some have claimed that they were written merely to convey wise sayings and lessons. However, the Gospel writers themselves do not leave such an impression. For example, in Luke's introduction to his Gospel, he clearly states he "carefully investigated everything from the beginning" in order to "write an accurate account" (1:3 NLT). John makes a similar statement when he notes, "But these are written so that you may continue to believe that Jesus is the Messiah, the Son of God, and that by believing in him you will have life by the power of his name" (John 20:31 NLT).

Another important evidence test—arguably one of the most difficult for ancient writers to pass—is known as the *adverse witness test.* With this test, scholars look at what the critics of the writer had to say. Did those critics admit the stories carried truthful details? What arguments did they offer to counter the claims of the writer?

Did they try to dismantle the author's premise? Did they try to sidestep the logical conclusion?

Scholar Craig Blomberg notes that some Jewish writers claimed Jesus was a sorcerer who led Israel astray.[17] This is a fascinating observation, as these writers could have claimed the miracles *never happened* or that the stories were all legendary tales that were made up. However, the fact that the enemies of Christianity needed to call Jesus a sorcerer provides reason to believe that something miraculous did indeed happen.

How would you describe the *intention test*? What does it seek to show about an author's intent behind his or her writing?

Based on the evidence, do you think the stories of Jesus recorded in the Gospels were written to convey wise sayings or something more? Explain.

What is the *adverse witness test*? Why is it the most difficult test for ancient writers to pass?

Many Jewish writers claimed that Jesus was a sorcerer who was leading the people of Israel astray. How does this actually serve to *support* the claims made in the Gospels?

Do you think the internal evidence text, the bibliographical test, or the external evidence test is the most powerful in proving the reliability of the New Testament? Why?

❺ Tacitus and Josephus
Evidence That Demands a Verdict, pages 83, 150, 153

Critics who doubt the historical accuracy of the New Testament often charge or imply that the accounts within its pages are unreliable because they were written by disciples of Jesus or later Christians. They sometimes claim there is *no* confirmation of Jesus or New Testament events recorded in non-Christian sources. However, we know of at least two non-Christian writers from antiquity who support accounts documented in the New Testament.

The first of these authors, Cornelius Tacitus, was a Roman historian who lived between AD 56 and 120. Theologian Robert Van Voorst says Tacitus "is generally considered the greatest Roman historian" and that his *Annals,* a history of the Roman Empire from the beginning of Tiberius's reign (AD 14) to the end of Nero's reign (AD 68), is his "finest work and generally acknowledged by modern historians as our best source of information about this period."[18]

Tacitus reports that in AD 64, a devastating fire broke out in Rome for which many believed Nero was responsible. In order to put a stop to the public outcry, Nero blamed the Christians. As Tacitus writes: "Therefore, to squelch the rumor, Nero created scapegoats and subjected to the most refined tortures those whom the common people called 'Christians' . . . Their name comes from Christ, who, during the reign of Tiberius, had been executed by the procurator Pontius Pilate. Suppressed for the moment, the deadly superstition broke out again, not only in Judea, the land which originated this evil, but also in the city of Rome."[19]

The second historian, Flavius Josephus, was a Jewish politician, soldier, and historian who lived around AD 37–100. He was born in Jerusalem shortly after the death of Jesus. His father was a respected high priest named Matthias, which not only places Josephus in Jerusalem right at the time the book of Acts says the new Christian church was flourishing there, but he would have been in a family that would have been acutely aware of a new religious movement that was seen as a threat to Judaism.[20]

According to theologians Greg Boyd and Paul R. Eddy, "[Josephus] is the single most important Jewish historian of the ancient world."[21] In *Antiquities of the Jews,* which Josephus wrote to explain the Jewish people and their beliefs to the Romans, he writes about the death of Jesus' brother James: "[The high priest] Ananus . . . assembled the Sanhedrin of judges, and brought before them the brother of Jesus, who was called Christ, whose name was James, and some others . . . he delivered them to be stoned."[22] Josephus thus verifies a man named James was put to death, that he was Jesus' brother, and this Jesus was called the Christ.

Do you find it surprising that some people today question whether Jesus was an actual person in history? Why or why not?

How does Tacitus's account of the fire that broke out in Rome in AD 64 support the claim that Jesus and the Christians actually existed during the first century?

Read John 19:5–16. What does Tacitus say about Christ? How does his account support the events that John reports of Jesus' execution in his Gospel?

Who was Flavius Josephus? What makes him especially qualified to report on the events taking place in first-century Palestine?

Read Mark 6:3, Acts 15:12–21, and Galatians 1:13–19. What do these accounts state about James? How does Josephus support these claims in his statement about James's death?

Recommended Reading

Use the space below to write any key insights or questions from your personal study that you want to discuss at the next group meeting. In preparation for next week, you may wish to review chapters 10 and 11 in *Evidence That Demands a Verdict*.

DID JESUS ACTUALLY RISE FROM THE DEAD?

Moreover, brethren, I declare to you the gospel which
I preached to you, which also you received and in which you stand,
by which also you are saved, if you hold fast that word which
I preached to you—unless you believed in vain. For I delivered to you
first of all that which I also received: that Christ died for our sins
according to the Scriptures, and that He was buried,
and that He rose again the third day according to the Scriptures.

1 CORINTHIANS 15:1–4

Welcome

The resurrection is the central event of the Christian faith. It is impossible to overstate its relevance. The resurrection of Jesus and Christianity either stand together . . . or they fall apart. As the apostle Paul summed it up in his first letter to the believers in Corinth, if Jesus did not rise from the dead, then nothing else matters in terms of our resurrection, the church, or Christianity. For this reason, we need to examine the evidence for the resurrection.

Perhaps the best place to begin this discussion is by defining what is actually meant by the term *resurrection*. In his groundbreaking historical analysis of the resurrection, scholar and theologian N. T. Wright explains how the word *resurrection* was used and what it meant to those living in the ancient world, whether they believed in the resurrection or not:

> This basic tenet of human existence and experience is accepted as axiomatic throughout the ancient world; once people have gone by the road of death, they do not return. . . . "Resurrection" was not one way of describing what death consisted of. It was a way of describing something everyone knew did not happen: the idea that death could be reversed, undone, could (as it were) work backwards. Not even in myth was it permitted.[1]

Wright points out that various ancient cultures all knew what the word *resurrection* meant—even if they did not all believe that it was something that would actually happen. It is important to remember that in no ancient culture did the term *resurrection* ever refer to anything other than bodily resurrection. A nonbodily resurrection would have been just as illogical as a square circle or a married bachelor.

In the Old and New Testaments, we find a total of nine (possibly ten) individuals and one group who were raised from the dead.

All of these people were brought back to life through God's power and ultimately died again. But Jesus rose from the dead in his own strength and possessed a perfect resurrection body that would *never* die again. He is the "firstfruit" of the future resurrection that is coming for all believers (see 1 Corinthians 15:23).

In this session, we will examine the historical evidence that supports the claim that Jesus rose from the dead, setting it in its proper historical context of first-century Jerusalem life.[2]

Share

Begin your group time by inviting anyone to share his or her insights from last week's personal study. Next, discuss one of the following questions:

- What questions do you have when you read the accounts in the Gospels of Jesus' crucifixion and resurrection from the dead?

— or —

- How did the people in the first century view resurrection? Why is it important to note the term never referred to anything other than *bodily* resurrection?

Read

Invite someone to read aloud the following passage from 1 Corinthians 15:12–19. Listen for fresh insight and then share any new thoughts with the group using the questions that follow.

Now if Christ is preached that He has been raised from the dead, how do some among you say that there is no resurrection of the dead? But if there is no resurrection of the dead, then Christ is not risen. And if Christ is not risen, then our preaching is empty and your faith is also empty. Yes, and we are found false witnesses of God, because we have testified of God that He raised up Christ, whom He did not raise up—if in fact the dead do not rise. For if the dead do not rise, then Christ is not risen. And if Christ is not risen, your faith is futile; you are still in your sins! Then also those who have fallen asleep in Christ have perished. If in this life only we have hope in Christ, we are of all men the most pitiable.

Paul provides a compelling either/or argument for the resurrection of Jesus. What are the only two options that he presents? What is the logical conclusion of each stance?

Why did Paul say his preaching (and our faith) would be empty if Jesus hadn't risen from the dead? Would the moral teachings of Jesus still stand and help us live good lives even if there was no resurrection? Explain.

On the other hand, if the resurrection of Jesus is real, what does that mean for both those who have already "fallen asleep in Christ" and those of us still living?

Watch

Play the video for session four. As you watch, use the following outline to record any thoughts or concepts that stand out to you.

Notes

The resurrection is either the most vicious, wicked, heartless hoax ever foisted upon the minds of men and women today . . . or it is the most fantastic fact of history.

Christianity hinges on the resurrection. The apostle Paul emphasizes that if Jesus wasn't raised from the dead, then our faith is in vain (see 1 Corinthians 15:12–19).

Jesus actually died. When Christ was stabbed with a spear, blood and water flowed from his body (see John 19:34). Medical experts verify that a water-like substance surrounds the pericardial sac of the heart in a crucified victim. When that sac is pierced, blood and water pour out.

Jesus' burial is also a crucial piece of evidence. All four Gospels are unified in saying Joseph of Arimathea buried him. He was part of the Sanhedrin—the group that condemned Jesus to death. Why would the apostles invent a heroic figure from the party that killed Jesus?

The fact that Jesus' tomb was empty was not in dispute at the time. The Jewish religious leaders accused the disciples of stealing Jesus' body, which was a concession his body was gone.

One popular theory states that people were just hallucinating when they witnessed Jesus alive after the crucifixion. But there is no scientific evidence for group hallucinations that mirror the account of Jesus appearing to groups of people that we find in the New Testament.

THE CASE FOR THE EMPTY TOMB

We may insist, in fact, that whatever else had happened, if the body of Jesus of Nazareth had remained in the tomb there would have been no early Christian belief of the sort we have discovered. It will not do to suggest, for instance, that because the disciples lived in a world where resurrection was expected, this will explain why they used that language of Jesus. Many other Jewish leaders, heroes and would-be Messiahs died within the same world, but in no case did anyone suggest that they had been raised from the dead. One might imagine other kinds of early faith which could have been generated by events which did not involve an empty tomb. But the specific faith of the earliest Christians could not have been generated by a set of circumstances in which an empty tomb did not play a part. I therefore regard the empty tomb as a necessary condition . . . for the rise of the very specific early Christian belief.[3]

—N.T. WRIGHT

Discuss

Take a few minutes with your group members to discuss what you just watched and explore these concepts in Scripture.

1. Throughout the Bible, we find stories of people who were raised from the dead. How did Jesus' resurrection differ from these other resurrections in Scripture?

2. Some critics claim that Jesus did not really die—that he just went into a swoon or faked his own death. What evidence from the Gospels reveal that Jesus was actually dead?

3. Read Mark 15:42–47. Who was Joseph of Arimathea? Why is it unlikely the Gospel writers would invent a figure like Joseph to be the one who buried Jesus?

4. Why would Jerusalem have been the most difficult place for the disciples to proclaim Jesus' resurrection from the dead if it wasn't true?

5. Read Mark 16:1–5. Each Gospel reports that it was women who discovered Jesus' tomb to be empty. How does this add credibility to the Gospel accounts of the resurrection?

6. An empty tomb could be explained naturally or supernaturally. What is the best piece of evidence that proves Jesus rose from the dead? Why did this become one of the most compelling reasons that people at the time believed Jesus was the Messiah?

Respond

In the Old Testament, God warned his people to beware of false prophets. At one point, as previously discussed, he even provided his people with a test to determine whether a certain prophet spoke for him (see Deuteronomy 18:22). Given this, if Jesus had made a claim that did not end up coming to pass, the people of his day would have seen him as a fraud and a liar. This is significant because several times in the Gospels, Jesus makes the assertion that he would be put to death but would rise again. Today, close out your time by selecting two of the passages listed below, and then write down some of the specific things Jesus says and/or instructs his disciples to do after he makes each prediction.

Verse(s)	Jesus' Words or Instructions
Matthew 17:9	
Matthew 17:22–23	
Matthew 20:18–19	
Matthew 26:32	

Verse(s)	Jesus' Words or Instructions
Mark 9:10	
Luke 9:22–27	
John 2:18–22	

Pray

Wrap up your time by taking a few moments to pray together. Here are a few ideas of what you could pray about based on the topics of this session:

- Ask God to make the resurrection of Jesus even more real to you.
- Express your gratitude for Jesus' death and resurrection for your sins.
- Pray that God will give you opportunities this week to share the message of salvation with others.
- Pray to live with a vibrant hope for both this life and the next because Jesus has shown you that death no longer has the final word.

BETWEEN-SESSIONS
PERSONAL STUDY

Reflect on the material you've covered this week by engaging in any or all of the following between-sessions activities. Each day offers a short reading from *Evidence That Demands a Verdict*, along with a few reflection questions to take you deeper into the theme of this week's study. Journal or write down your thoughts after each question. At the start of the next session, you will have a few minutes to share any insights you learned.

❶ The Meaning of *Resurrection*
Evidence That Demands a Verdict, pages 43, 233–234

The earliest resurrection narrative is likely recorded in Mark 16:1–8. According to church tradition, Mark was an associate of Peter, and it is likely that the witness of Peter was the source of Mark's content. If this is the case, it would mean that Mark wrote the Gospel from AD 50–60, before Peter was martyred in AD 64. Mark, a bilingual Hellenist, might have written his Gospel to encourage Christians in Rome and other parts of the world.

In writing his Gospel, Mark certainly recognized that both Jews and non-Jews were familiar with the term *resurrection*. There was a common definition, though there was no consensus regarding its reality. As N. T. Wright states, "Here there is no difference between pagans, Jews and Christians. They all understood the Greek word *anastasis* and its *cognates*, and the other related terms we shall meet, to mean . . . new life after a period of being dead. Pagans denied this possibility; some Jews affirmed it as a long-term future hope; virtually all Christians claimed that it had happened to Jesus and would happen to them in the future."[4]

Bolstering his assertion, Wright explains the importance to the Greek and Roman world of *embodiment* in relation to the concept of *resurrection*:

> The meaning of "resurrection," both in Jewish and the non-Jewish world of late antiquity, was never that the person concerned had simply "gone to heaven," or been "exalted" in some way which did not involve a new bodily life. Plenty of disembodied postmortem states were postulated, and there was a rich variety of terminology for denoting them, which did not include "resurrection." "Resurrection" meant embodiment; that was equally so for the pagans, who denied it, as it was for the Jews, at least some of whom hoped for it.[5]

Again, in no ancient culture did "resurrection" ever refer to anything other than bodily resurrection. A nonbodily resurrection would have seemed illogical to everyone.

Compare Mark 16:1–8 with Matthew 28:1–11 and Luke 21:1–12. What similarities do you notice in each of these accounts?

What differences do you notice in each of these accounts?

What did the term *resurrection* mean to those living in the first-century world?

N. T. Wright states that *"Resurrection* was . . . the idea that death could be reversed, undone, could (as it were) work backwards. Not even in myth was it permitted." Why do you suppose this was a forbidden concept—especially in the Jewish culture?

In ancient cultures, the term *resurrection* never referred to anything other than a literal bodily resurrection. How does this discredit modern skeptics who say Jesus' resurrection, if it happened at all, was only spiritual in nature?

Resuscitation Versus Resurrection
Evidence That Demands a Verdict, pages 234–235

As previously noted, the Bible records a total of nine individuals and one group who were raised from the dead. What sets Jesus' resurrection apart from the other miraculous events of dead people being brought back to life? As Paul explains, "But now Christ is risen from the dead, and has become the firstfruits of those who have fallen asleep. . . . For as in Adam all die, even so in Christ all shall be made alive. But each one in his own order: Christ the firstfruits, afterward those who are Christ's at His coming" (1 Corinthians 15:20, 22–23).

Paul says Jesus is the *firstfruits* of those who are resurrected. But what about those who were raised *before* his resurrection? What about those in the Old Testament or the ones whom Jesus raised? Wouldn't they be the firstfruits? Not according to Paul. Jesus was resurrected—never to die again. All the others who were brought back to life were raised, *but eventually died again*—to be raised a final time with those who belong to Christ at his Second Coming. The quality of their resurrection was something different from the one Jesus experienced.

In addition, Jesus' resurrected body had *new characteristics* that his pre-resurrection body had not possessed. He was able to appear and disappear at will (see Luke 24:31, 36–37, 51; John 20:19, 26), and he ascended to heaven in his physical body (see Acts 1:6–11). None of the others who were raised had yet received their new resurrected bodies—they were raised in their mortal flesh-and-blood bodies in which they had previously died. This is why their resurrections are really *resuscitations*, while Jesus was resurrected in the fullest sense.

Jesus was not the first person in the Bible to be raised from the dead (see 1 Kings 17:17–24; 2 Kings 4:35; 13:21). But what set Jesus' resurrection apart from any other biblical example?

According to the apostle Paul, how does the term *firstfruits* apply to Jesus' resurrection?

Why wouldn't those raised from the dead in the Old Testament, or the people Jesus raised, be considered "firstfruits," since those occurrences happened prior to Jesus' resurrection?

Read Luke 24:31–37, 51 and John 20:19–26. What two new characteristics did Jesus' resurrected body possess?

What is the critical difference between *resuscitation* and *resurrection*?

❸ The Center of New Testament Theology
Evidence That Demands a Verdict, page 238

So much of what Christians believe is connected directly to the resurrection of Jesus of Nazareth. In Paul's letters, he explicitly links believers' forgiveness, salvation, and resurrection to Jesus' resurrection. He also indicates the comprehensive range of what God has done and will do, especially since the Greek word translated *salvation* conveys a wonderful array of meanings—rescue, deliverance, safety, defense, and wholeness:

> If you confess with your mouth the Lord Jesus and believe in your heart that God has raised Him from the dead, you will be saved. For with the heart one believes unto righteousness, and with the mouth confession is made unto salvation (Romans 10:9–10).

He who raised up the Lord Jesus will also raise us up with Jesus, and will present us with you (2 Corinthians 4:14).

For if we believe that Jesus died and rose again, even so God will bring with Him those who sleep in Jesus (1 Thessalonians 4:14).

Adrian Warnock, a church leader, author, and clinical psychiatrist, writes on the topic of Christian theology and practice as it pertains to the resurrection. Drawing on the book of Acts, he reveals how several Christian doctrines are based on the resurrection, including the sending of the Spirit (2:33), physical healings (3:15–16), salvation by union with Jesus (4:11–12), Jesus' role as the leader of his church (5:30–31), forgiveness of sins (5:30–31), commissioning of the gospel messengers (10:42), and assurance the gospel is true (17:31).

Furthermore, Jesus' resurrection provides assurance of our own resurrection at his Second Coming and points to his future judgment of this world. "He has appointed a day on which He will judge the world in righteousness by the Man whom He has ordained. He has given assurance of this to all by raising Him from the dead" (17:31).[6]

Before now, have you considered how Jesus' resurrection is at the center of all New Testament theology? Can you now make the case for why that is true?

How does the resurrection make possible for believers in Christ forgiveness from sin, salvation, and our own resurrection one day?

In 1 Corinthians 15:19, Paul states that "if our hope in Christ is only for this life, we are more to be pitied than anyone in the world" (NLT). Why is Paul so adamant about this point?

The resurrection of Jesus accomplished far more than many people realize. What are at least four doctrines of the church that are based on the resurrection?

Which of these especially resonate with you? Why?

❹ Post-Resurrection Appearances of Jesus
Evidence That Demands a Verdict, pages 263–264

The disciples' claim that they encountered a physical, resurrected Jesus was not an idea they would have borrowed from anyone else. It did not arise from within their own belief system. Philosopher Douglas Groothuis summarizes this point well:

> [The] Second Temple Judaism of Jesus' day had no concept of disembodied resurrection. Those Jews who believed in the afterlife . . . believed in a general resurrection of all people at the end of history. . . . Therefore, Jesus' resurrection differed from the prevailing view in that (1) it happened in

history, not at the end of history, and (2) it happened to one individual, not to the entire human race. Given this, the early church could not have derived their idea of Jesus' singular resurrection in history from prevailing Jewish ideas. Thus if Jesus' followers (or others) had only visionary or apparitional experiences of Jesus, these would not have supported the claim that he was alive. . . . They could at best claim that Jesus' disembodied spirit was making various appearances on earth. But the New Testament nowhere makes this claim, since it emphasizes the physical resurrection of Jesus and the empty tomb.[7]

Scholar N. T. Wright concurs with this statement, adding, "[If] a first-century Jew said that someone had been 'raised from the dead,' the one thing they did not mean was that such a person had gone to a state of disembodied bliss, there either to rest forever or to wait until the great day of re-embodiment."[8]

Both Groothuis and Wright get at the same point. If Jesus was indeed resurrected, it was a *physical* Jesus the disciples saw and interacted with in some *physical* way. It was radically different from the disembodied continuation-after-death that appears in other ancient documents in the Greek and Roman world—including in the works of Plato, Homer, and Virgil. But the New Testament insists in a bold and historically reliable way on a resurrection that is bodily. Jesus was not just a spirit. The term *resurrection* was not just a figure of speech.

Read Matthew 22:23–33. What does Jesus have to say about the resurrected life?

Read Daniel 12:2. What does this verse state about resurrection?

There are two ways that Jesus' resurrection differed from the prevailing view of his times. What was the first way it different?

What was the second way Jesus' resurrection went counter to prevailing Jewish ideas?

Why is it true that if Jesus' followers (or others) had only *visionary* or *apparitional* experiences of him, it would not have supported their claim that he was alive?

⑤ Is Christianity a Copycat Religion?
Evidence That Demands a Verdict, pages 304–309, 314

The regions surrounding the Mediterranean world gave birth to several mystery religions and cults. Because these religions were practiced during the formative years of Christianity, questions arose: *Did early Christians borrow certain rituals and concepts from these pagan religions to make Christianity more appealing to potential converts? Did Christianity plagiarize these mystery religions? Are there any aspects genuinely unique to Christianity?*

We have limited information about the mystery religions (partly because of a vow of secrecy imposed on the initiates), but we do know that none of the so-called resurrect gods in these religions *was a historical figure*. In contrast, Jesus is depicted in the Bible as a real historical person. The Gospel accounts contain many anchors that hold in place, so to speak, vessels full of evidential treasures for anyone to examine, especially for those who wonder about the truth of Christianity.

In addition, the mystery religions held *secret ceremonies*. The rites the practitioners participated in and the knowledge they passed to their initiates were closely guarded, accessible only to those who were accepted into the group. In sharp contrast, Christianity was a very public religion . . . so much so that it often got its adherents into serious trouble. For instance, the book of Acts records that at one point the apostles were threatened, beaten, and put in prison for publicly proclaiming the gospel (see 4:1–3; 5:17–42).

Finally, the mystery religions placed *little emphasis on doctrine*. They were less concerned about having correct teaching than in feeding the emotions of their followers. In contrast, the Christian Scriptures place a high importance on teaching and believing (see Deuteronomy 11:11–23, Matthew 28:18–20, and Titus 1:9).

The resurrection of Jesus was a unique event in world history. It was not a "copycat" religion, and there is certainly no compelling reason to think the first Christians borrowed concepts from the mystery religions to concoct their faith.

What are some claims in recent years that skeptics have made about the birth of Christianity?

How does Christianity differ from the mystery religions in terms of its central figure? What do the Gospels claim about Jesus in this regard?

How does Christianity differ from the mystery religions in terms of the way its ceremonies and gatherings were conducted?

How does Christianity differ from the mystery religions in terms of its emphasis on doctrine?

At most, there are only vague hints of gods in the mystery religions who visit humankind, die, and rise to bring them to victory. Given this, why do you think the "copycat" theories continue to prevail in popular culture?

Recommended Reading

Use the space below to write any key insights or questions from your personal study that you want to discuss at the next group meeting. In preparation for next week, you may wish to review chapters 7–9 and 12 in *Evidence That Demands a Verdict*.

DID JESUS CLAIM TO BE GOD?

Now Jesus and His disciples went out to the towns of Caesarea
Philippi; and on the road He asked His disciples, saying to them,
"Who do men say that I am?" So they answered, "John the Baptist;
but some say, Elijah; and others, one of the prophets." He said to them,
"But who do you say that I am?" Peter answered and said to Him,
"You are the Christ." Then He strictly warned them that
they should tell no one about Him.

MARK 8:27–30

Welcome

One time, when Jesus was walking with his disciples in the region of Caesarea Philippi, he turned to them and asked, "Who do men say that I am?" (Mark 8:27). The question was surprising on many levels. For one, it was typically the disciple, not the rabbi, who asked the questions. Also, Jesus certainly already knew the answer, for he had been with the crowds and heard what they were saying about him. But as the conversation unfolds, it becomes clear that Jesus did not ask the question to gain information. He had a greater purpose.[1]

The answers the disciples gave indicated both the high regard that people held for Jesus and how divided their opinions were about him. Some said he was John the Baptist risen from the dead (see Matthew 14:2). Others saw him as Elijah, a forerunner to a Messiah who was still to come (see Malachi 4:5–6), or Jeremiah, or one of the other prophets of old (see Matthew 16:14). Jesus listens to these responses—again, answers he would have already known—and then turns the question back to the disciples: "But who do you say that I am?" (Luke 9:20).[2]

The question reveals the controversy about Jesus that exists to this day. On the one hand, adherents of Christianity believe he is the divine Son of God, the fulfillment of ancient biblical prophecies, and the promised Savior of the world. On the other hand, skeptics contend Jesus was neither divine nor that he every claimed to be. For instance, Robert M. Price, a self-described atheist and Jesus Seminar fellow, has stated "there is zero evidence that Jesus claimed to be divine."[3] Renowned skeptic Bart Ehrman argues the concept of deity was ambiguous in Jesus' day, and that any such claims—if Jesus made them—are not to be taken as direct declarations of his divinity.[4]

So, which is it? Was Jesus a mere mortal—the loving, peace-making cult hero that many today make him out to be? Or was he more than human? Did Jesus claim to be God or only an earthly agent of God? How did his followers and other contemporaries perceive him? Where does the evidence point? Fortunately, the New Testament writers invite us to examine Jesus for *ourselves*—to ask the same question that Jesus posed to his disciples—and to discern his significance in our lives. In this session, we will look at this question of whether Jesus really *claimed* to be God, whether the Old Testament prophecies about the Messiah were actually fulfilled in him, and whether he truly is the divine Son of God.[5]

Share

Begin your group time by inviting anyone to share his or her insights from last week's personal study. Next, discuss one of the following questions:

- Do you agree there is "zero evidence" that Jesus actually claimed to be divine? Why or why not?

— *or* —

- Do you believe Jesus actually was God? Why or why not?

Read

Invite someone to read aloud the following passage from John 8:48–59. Listen for fresh insight and then share any new thoughts with the group using the questions that follow.

Then the Jews answered and said to Him, "Do we not say rightly that You are a Samaritan and have a demon?"

Jesus answered, "I do not have a demon; but I honor My Father, and you dishonor Me. And I do not seek My own glory; there is One who seeks and judges. Most assuredly, I say to you, if anyone keeps My word he shall never see death."

Then the Jews said to Him, "Now we know that You have a demon! Abraham is dead, and the prophets; and You say, 'If anyone keeps My word he shall never taste death.' Are You greater than our father Abraham, who is dead? And the prophets are dead. Who do You make Yourself out to be?"

Jesus answered, "If I honor Myself, My honor is nothing. It is My Father who honors Me, of whom you say that He is your God. Yet you have not known Him, but I know Him. And if I say, 'I do not know Him,' I shall be a liar like you; but I do know Him and keep His word. Your father Abraham rejoiced to see My day, and he saw it and was glad."

Then the Jews said to Him, "You are not yet fifty years old, and have You seen Abraham?"

Jesus said to them, "Most assuredly, I say to you, before Abraham was, I AM."

Then they took up stones to throw at Him; but Jesus hid Himself and went out of the temple, going through the midst of them, and so passed by.

What stands out to you about this passage?

Why do you think the religious leaders viewed Jesus' statement as blasphemy?

How is Jesus' comment similar to God telling Moses at the burning bush, "I AM WHO I AM" (Exodus 3:14)?

Watch

Play the video for session five. As you watch, use the following outline to record any thoughts or concepts that stand out to you.

Notes

Jesus was not shy or hesitant to proclaim his deity:

- Jesus claimed to be God during his trial before the high priest and Sanhedrin (see Mark 14).

- When Jesus asked his disciples who they thought he was, they said, "You are the Son of the living God." Jesus didn't rebuke them but responded, "My Father in Heaven is the one who revealed that to you" (see Mark 8:27–30).

- When Jesus spoke with the religious leaders of his day, he plainly stated, "Before Abraham was, I AM" (John 8:58).

Jesus also made statements that indirectly reveal his divine authority. For example, after healing a paralytic man, he said to him, "Your sins are forgiven you" (Mark 2:5).

Other people in the early church also claimed that Jesus was God, including the apostle Paul and the author of the book of Hebrews.

The "Trilemma" refers to a statement that C. S. Lewis made popular that states Jesus is either:

- A *liar* . . .

- A *lunatic* . . .

- Or the *Lord* . . .

The Old Testament, written over a period of about 1,000 years, contains approximately 260 major prophecies about the Messiah. They are all fulfilled in only *one* person—Jesus Christ.

The Greek translation of the Hebrew Old Testament—with all these prophecies of who the Messiah would be—was completed 150–200 years before Jesus was born.

. . . .

THE PROPHECY OF THE MESSIAH

In Genesis 3:15, God said the Messiah would be born of the Seed of the woman (the virgin birth). We can go through recorded time to find how God ultimately fulfilled this prophecy in Jesus:

- God eliminates two-thirds of the nations of the world when he selects the Messiah to come from the lineage of Shem (see Genesis 9:26–27).

- God eliminates every family from Shem's line except one when he chooses the Messiah to come from the descendants of Abraham (see Genesis 12:1–3).

- God eliminates seven-eighths of Abraham's line when he chooses the Messiah to come from the line of Isaac and Jacob (see Genesis 26:2–5; 35:9–12).

- God eliminates eleven-twelfths of the tribes of Israel when he selects the Messiah to come from the tribe of Judah (see Genesis 49:8–10).

- God eliminates every family in the tribe of Judah except one when he selects the Messiah to come from the family of Jesse (see 1 Samuel 16:11–13 and Isaiah 11:1–16).

- God eliminates seven-eighths of the family line of Jesse when he selects the Messiah to come from the house of David (see 2 Samuel 7:4–16).

- God further narrows this down c. 1012 BC when he says the Messiah will also be crucified—a form of execution that will not be implemented by the Romans until 800 years later (see Psalm 22:16–18).

- God then eliminates every city for the Messiah's entrance into the world except one—the tiny village of Bethlehem (see Micah 5:2).

- God further narrows this down when he says the Messiah will be betrayed by a friend for thirty pieces of silver (see Psalm 41:9 and Zechariah 11:13–14).

- God narrows this down even more when he says this will all take place before the destruction of the temple in AD 70 (see Daniel 9:24–27).

The prophecies in the Bible limit who could be the rightful Messiah . . . and only Jesus fulfills every one.[6]

· ·

Discuss

Take a few minutes with your group members to discuss what you just watched and explore these concepts in Scripture.

1. During Jesus' trial (see Mark 14), the high priest tore his garments after hearing from Jesus. What is the significance of this act?

2. When Jesus asks his disciples who they say he is, Peter replies, "You are the Messiah" (Mark 8:29 NLT). How did Jesus respond

to Peter's statement? How do these words confirm Jesus' view of his own deity?

3. When Jesus healed the paralytic who was lowered through the roof (see Mark 2), he said to the man, "Your sins are forgiven" (verse 5). Why would this upset the religious leaders? What do these four words reveal about the identity of Jesus?

4. In Titus 2:13, Paul says he is "looking for the blessed hope and glorious appearing of our great God and Savior Jesus Christ." Paul embraces Jesus as both eternal God and personal Savior. Do you struggle with this interpretation? Why or why not?

5. In Hebrews 1:8 we read, "Your throne, O God, is forever and ever; a scepter of righteousness is the scepter of Your kingdom." What do these words indicate about the writer of Hebrews' belief in Jesus being the Son of God?

6. C. S. Lewis popularized what is known as the "Trilemma of Jesus," or the idea that when it comes to Jesus' claims about himself, we must consider him either a *liar,* a *lunatic,* or the *Lord.* Which option seems to be the truest based on the evidence? What are the flaws with the idea Jesus was a liar or a lunatic?

Respond

When you are putting together a jigsaw puzzle, the numerous pieces scattered across the table can seem confusing until you assemble enough of the puzzle to get an idea of what the picture represents. In the same way, the numerous prophecies about the Messiah in the Old Testament can seem confusing until you begin to study and assemble them—and when you do, you find they reveal a picture of Christ in the New Testament. Today, close out your time by selecting two Old Testament prophecies from the list below that reveal information about the identity of the Messiah. Then look up the corresponding New Testament passage and briefly write down in your own words how Jesus fulfilled that prophecy.

Trait	Old Testament Prophecy	New Testament Fulfillment
Pre-existent	Micah 5:2: "Out of you shall come forth to Me the One to be Ruler in Israel, whose goings forth are from of old, from everlasting."	Colossians 1:17

Trait	Old Testament Prophecy	New Testament Fulfillment
Prophet	Deuteronomy 18:18: "I will raise up for them a Prophet like you from among their brethren, and will put My words in His mouth, and He shall speak to them all that I command Him."	Matthew 21:11
House of David	Isaiah 11:1–2: "There shall come forth a Rod from the stem of Jesse, and a Branch shall grow out of his roots. The Spirit of the LORD shall rest upon Him."	Romans 1:1–3:
Judge	Isaiah 33:22: "(For the LORD is our Judge, the LORD is our Lawgiver, the LORD is our King; He will save us.)"	2 Timothy 4:1

Trait	Old Testament Prophecy	New Testament Fulfillment
King	Psalm 2:6: "Yet I have set My King on My holy hill of Zion."	Matthew 27:37
Miracle Worker	Isaiah 35:5–6: "Then the eyes of the blind shall be opened, and the ears of the deaf shall be unstopped. Then the lame shall leap like a deer, and the tongue of the dumb sing."	Matthew 9:35
Teacher	Psalm 78:2: "I will open my mouth in a parable; I will utter dark sayings of old."	Matthew 13:34–35
Light to the Gentiles	Isaiah 49:6: "Indeed He says, 'It is too small a thing that You should be My Servant to raise up the tribes of Jacob, and to restore the preserved ones of Israel; I will also give You as a light to the Gentiles, that You should be My salvation to the ends of the earth.'"	Acts 13:47–48

Pray

Wrap up your time by taking a few moments to pray together. Here are a few ideas of what you could pray about based on the topics of this session:

- Proclaim your belief in Jesus as the Son of God.
- Thank God for coming to this world in human form.
- Thank God that he understands exactly what you are going through each day.
- Express your praise to God for revealing Jesus as the Messiah through the numerous Old Testament prophecies that he fulfilled.
- Ask God to help you know that he will be with you and beside you each day.

BETWEEN-SESSIONS PERSONAL STUDY

Reflect on the material you've covered this week by engaging in any or all of the following between-sessions activities. Each day offers a short reading from *Evidence That Demands a Verdict*, along with a few reflection questions to take you deeper into the theme of this week's study. Journal or write down your thoughts after each question. At the start of the next session, you will have a few minutes to share any insights you learned.

① Jesus Received Worship Reserved for God Alone
Evidence That Demands a Verdict, page 179

The Bible issues a persistent warning against worshiping anything or anyone but God himself. The first of the Ten Commandments states, "You shall have no other gods before Me" (Exodus 20:3). The Old Testament is filled with cautions against idolatry, admonitions to those engaging in the practice, warnings of grave consequences should they persist, and detailed descriptions of those consequences as they were experienced. The New Testament similarly warns people to "flee from idolatry" (1 Corinthians 10:14). In Matthew 4:10, Jesus declares worship should be restricted to God alone. He taught people to worship God "in spirit and truth" (John 4:19–24).

Jesus' disciples clearly understood this message. In the book of Acts, we read of Peter's reaction to someone's attempt to worship him: "As Peter was coming in, Cornelius met him and fell down at his feet and worshiped him. But Peter lifted him up, saying, 'Stand up; I myself am also a man'" (Acts 10:25–26). Later, we read of a similar encounter with the apostles Paul and Barnabas in Lystra:

> Now when the people saw what Paul had done, they raised up their voices, saying in the Lycaonian language, "The gods have come down to us in the likeness of men!" . . . But when the apostles Barnabas and Paul heard this, they tore their clothes and ran in among the multitude, crying out and saying, "Men, why are you doing these things? We also are men with the same nature as you, and preach to you that you should turn from these useless things to the living God" (Acts 14:11, 14–15).

From the above passages, we note that worship, one of the most common themes of the Bible, is suitable solely for God. Idolatry is an egregious offense. It is remarkable, then, to find that Jesus *freely accepted* worship.

Why do you think the Bible warns us against worshiping anyone or anything except God?

What are some of the "other things" that people worship?

Jesus knew this commandment, but the Bible revelas that he freely accepted worship. In fact, there are numerous New Testament examples where Jesus allowed others to worship him. Next to each reference below, write out the complete verse, and then add any thoughts or insights these passages provoke:

Matthew 14:33

Matthew 28:9

John 9:38

On these occasions, did Jesus correct anyone for worshiping him? Why or why not?

Not only did Jesus accept worship during his first-century ministry, but the New Testament also alludes to current and future worship of Jesus. For each reference below, write out the complete verse, and then add any thoughts or insights these passages provoke:

Hebrews 1:6

Revelation 5:14

Why do you think the disciples (and the everyday people) had less trouble accepting who Jesus was than the religious and political leaders of that time?

❷ Jesus' Followers Believed He Was God
Evidence That Demands a Verdict, page 181

The apostle Paul said of Jesus, "He is the image of the invisible God, the first-born of all creation. For by him all things were created, in heaven and on earth, visible and invisible, whether thrones or dominions or rulers or authorities—all things were created through him and for him. And he is before all things, and in him all things hold together" (Colossians 1:15–17 ESV). Paul ascribed attributes of deity to Jesus, asserting that even though God the Father is unseen, his image and likeness have been conveyed through Jesus.

Wheaton College scholar Christopher Beetham explains, "The phrase 'image of the invisible God' expresses the same idea as Hebrews 1:3, that the Son 'is the radiance of the glory of God and the exact imprint of his nature.'"[7] Writer and speaker Peter Lewis adds, "What [Jesus represents] he must also possess; he [represents] God's real being precisely because he shares that real being. As the image of God, Jesus Christ is God's equivalent in the world of men."[8] This explanation is so important to grasp because our modern culture has forgotten how to think of the spiritual as truly real. Jesus conveys the glory of God because he *is* God.

Paul then credits Jesus with a central role in creation, stating that all things were created by him, through him, and for him. Professor of theology Stephen Wellum notes this passage is "consistent with other New Testament texts that attribute the divine work of creation to the Son, thus teaching his deity."[9] Beetham adds, "Paul writes that not only is the Son the agent *through* whom God created all things, but he is also the *goal* or purpose for which they all exist."[10]

In Colossians 1:15, Paul says Jesus is the image of the invisible God. Given that God doesn't have a human form, what do you think the word *image* here means?

In Philippians 2:6–7, Paul refers to Jesus as the one "who, being in the form of God, did not consider it robbery to be equal with God, but made Himself of no reputation, taking the form of a bondservant, and coming in the likeness of men." How does this statement of Christ's pre-existence impact your view of Jesus' thirty-three years of life on earth?

Read 2 Peter 1:1. What is the dual phrase that Peter uses to describe Jesus? Why is this description significant?

Read John 20:28. After Jesus' resurrection, Christ invited his disciple Thomas to touch his wounds. When Thomas did, what did he cry out? Although Jesus rebuked Thomas for his unbelief, how did he respond to this comment?

The apostle John writes, "In the beginning was the Word and the Word was with God, and the Word was God. . . . And the Word became flesh and dwelt among us" (John 1:1, 14). Who is "the Word"? What is the Word's relationship to God?

❸ Jesus Was Either a Liar, a Lunatic, or the Lord
Evidence That Demands a Verdict, pages 196, 198

What did Jesus believe about himself? How did others perceive him? *Who is Jesus of Nazareth?* Jesus thought it was fundamentally important what others believed about him. It was not a subject that allowed for neutrality or a less-than-honest appraisal of the evidence. C. S. Lewis captured this truth in his book *Mere Christianity*. After surveying some of the evidence regarding Jesus' identity, Lewis wrote:

> I am trying here to prevent anyone saying the really foolish thing that people often say about him: I'm ready to accept Jesus as a great moral teacher, but I don't accept his claim to be God. That is the one thing we must not say. A man who was merely a man and said the sort of things Jesus said would not be a great moral teacher. He would either be a lunatic—on the level with the man who says he is a poached egg—or else he would be the Devil of Hell. You must make your choice. Either this man was, and is, the Son of God, or else a madman or something worse. You can shut him up for a fool, you can spit at him and kill him as a demon or you can fall at his feet and call him Lord and God, but let us not come with any patronizing nonsense about his

being a great human teacher. He has not left that open to us. He did not intend to.[11]

Jesus' claim to be God must be either true or false. If it is true, then he is the *Lord,* and our only choice is to accept or reject him. But if Jesus' claims to be God were false, then we are left with just two options: either he knew his claims were false and was a *liar,* or he didn't know they were false and was a *lunatic.*

If Jesus knew he was not God, then he was not just lying but also unspeakably evil. Do you think it is possible for a liar of this magnitude to leave us with the most profound ethical truths and morally exemplary life as Jesus did? Why or why not?

J Warner Wallace, a cold-case homicide detective featured on *Dateline* and *Court TV,* lists three motives that lie at the heart of any deception: (1) financial greed, (2) sexual or relational desire, and (3) pursuit of power. Is there a good reason to think Jesus was led to lie by any of these three motives? Why or why not?

If Jesus was deluded, he would be the most delusional person who ever lived. He believed he was God, persuaded others to follow him, and died for that cause. What aspects of his story reveal that he was connected to reality and did not display tendencies of a madman?

If Jesus is neither a liar nor lunatic, can you think of another viable option for what he could be other than Lord? Give it your creative best shot. If you cannot think of another option, why do you suppose so many refuse to believe that Jesus is Lord?

It has been said that some reject the clear evidence of Jesus as Lord because of moral implications. What are several moral reasons that may cause people to resist accepting Jesus as Lord? What would your response be to each objection?

❹ Jesus Fulfilled Old Testament Prophecies

Evidence That Demands a Verdict, pages 206, 212

The New Testament is the decryption key for unlocking the meaning of the prophecies concerning the Messiah in the Old Testament. This often plays out through a narrative text, where a detail or element hints at some larger idea while remaining a real part of its own story. Centuries of biblical interpreters have followed the lead of the authors of Scripture, who quote the Old Testament to emphasize and explain a detail that they believe points to Christ. For instance, Paul does so in Galatians 4, transferring the ideas of slavery and freedom in the history of Hagar and Sarah to the freedom given through Christ (see Galatians 4:21–5:1)

The authors of Scripture make these kinds of connections by recognizing a fundamental and theological unity between the element's meaning in the initial narrative and its meaning in the life or work of Christ. The image or other element in the Old Testament is called a *type*; it foreshadows or prefigures what the New Testament says. In a sense, a type acts like a prophecy. Interpretation using this method must take care to be faithful to the original narrative, letting the meaning arise from the element's real function in the Old Testament.

How does the New Testament act as a "decryption key" for unlocking the meaning of Old Testament Scriptures?

In Exodus 12:21, Moses tells the elders of Israel to select and kill a Passover lamb for the sins of their families. Read that verse and then turn to 1 Corinthians 5:7. How does Jesus fulfill this prophecy in the New Testament?

The Old Testament tells little about a mysterious figure named Melchizedek (see Genesis 14:17–20 and Psalm 110:4). We do know that he is one of only two people in the Bible who simultaneously held the title of priest and king. Read Hebrews 7:1–3. What insights does this passage provide into who Melchizedek represents?

In the desert, God commanded Moses to make a bronze serpent and set it on a pole. Anyone who was bitten by a poisonous snake could look on it and be delivered from death (see Numbers 21:8–9). In what way does this prophecy reach fulfillment in John 3:14–15?

Jesus' favorite self-designation in the Gospels is the title "Son of Man" (Mark 14: 62). How does the prophetic text of Daniel 7:13–14 foreshadow this significant name for Jesus?

⑤ Investigating the Deity of Jesus
Evidence That Demands a Verdict, page 358

There are two rival hypotheses about the life of Jesus. The first hypothesis states that Jesus was a good teacher, perhaps something of a prophet, who ran afoul of the political authorities and was executed. As the years passed following his death, legends developed about how he had performed miracles and rose from the dead— and even that he was born of a virgin. These legendary elements eventually led to the belief that Jesus was God incarnate. In short, the early church invented claims of deity for Jesus and the stories that supported those claims.

The second hypothesis states that Jesus was a teacher but an extraordinary one, performing miracles that astounded the people. He also made divine claims for himself in connection with these miracles that the Jewish authorities considered blasphemous. They had him arrested and handed over to the Roman authorities, who crucified him as a potential threat to order. He then rose from the dead, appeared to his followers, and ascended to heaven. The community of believers whom he left behind, which included members of his family, preserved their recollections of the things that Jesus had said and done. His family passed on to others their own stories, including that Jesus' mother Mary was a virgin when he was born.

As the early church reflected on what they knew about Jesus, they understood he was the Son of God who had come down from heaven. In short, the early church accepted Jesus' claims to deity in light of the evidence that supported those claims—especially his resurrection.

Which of the above two hypotheses about Jesus is best supported by the evidence? Give an example based on what you have learned so far in this study.

Many modern skeptics don't believe Jesus performed miracles. Yet, ironically, his miracles were conceded by most Jewish people in the first century and beyond. What does Mark 3:22 reveal about their explanation for his miracles?

If the holy, morally perfect God were to become incarnate as a human being, one would reasonably expect he would live a good and righteous life. What do the following passages say about the life of Jesus?

Luke 4:1–13

Acts 3:13–14

Hebrews 1:9

Revelation 3:7

Jesus' followers viewed him as sinless, but the question has been raised as to whether Jesus viewed *himself* in that way. Read John 5:19 and John 8:29, 46. Which phrases in these verses shed light on how Jesus viewed himself?

When Jesus hung on the cross, the people said, "He saved others; Himself He cannot save" (Matthew 27:42). Read Matthew 26:53–54. How does Jesus address this idea that he could not save himself? Why did Jesus choose to endure the pain of the cross?

Recommended Reading

Use the space below to write any key insights or questions from your personal study that you want to discuss at the next group meeting. In preparation for next week, you may wish to review chapters 4–5 in *Evidence That Demands a Verdict*.

HOW DO WE KNOW THE BIBLE IS ACCURATE?

And we know that all things work together for good to those
who love God, to those who are the called according to His purpose.
For whom He foreknew, He also predestined to be conformed to
the image of His Son, that He might be the firstborn
among many brethren.

ROMANS 8:28–29

Welcome

When it comes to the common objections that people have against Christianity, one of the major arguments that often surfaces is that the Bible is not reliable. This question is not only related to how we can know that what we have in our Bibles today is what was originally written down—as was discussed in a previous session—but also whether we have the *correct* books in the Bible and whether we can *trust* its teachings. In this respect, one criticism in particular that people raise about the Bible (and God, for that matter) is the issue of *evil and suffering* in the world. Scholar Bart Ehrman summarized this problem when he wrote:

> The big issue that drove me to agnosticism has to do not with the Bible, but with the pain and suffering in the world. I eventually found it impossible to explain the existence of evil so rampant among us—whether in terms of genocides (which continue), unspeakable human cruelty, war, disease, hurricanes, tsunamis, mudslides, the starvation of millions of innocent children, you name it—if there was a good and loving God who was actively involved in this world. For me to come to believe again, I would need to understand how there can be a God given a world such as this.[1]

Evil and suffering are perhaps *the* most powerful reasons why people struggle with the idea of God. After all, who has not at some point looked at the world and cried out, like the prophet Habakkuk, "O LORD, how long shall I cry, and You will not hear? Even cry out to You, 'Violence!' and You will not save?" (Habakkuk 1:2).

In this final session, we will look at some of the most common objections that both Christians and non-Christians raise when it comes to the reliability of the Bible. We will examine how the Old Testament was copied over the centuries and how we can trust it today. We will look at some of the "other" books that did not make it into our modern-day Bibles—such as the "secret" gospels—and how we can know that the text we have today represents God's own word. And, of course, we will examine the big issue of sin and suffering in our world.[2]

Share

Begin your group time by inviting anyone to share his or her insights from last week's personal study. Next, discuss one of the following questions:

- What big question about faith, the Bible, or God do you still wrestle with today? Are you willing to discuss it with the group and seek their input?

— *or* —

- Apologetics isn't just about knowing truth . . . it's also about applying those truths relationally in all aspects of your life. With whom will you share the truths you have learned in this study? When might that happen?

Read

Invite someone to read aloud the following passage from 2 Timothy 3:10–17. Listen for fresh insight and then share any new thoughts with the group using the questions that follow.

But you have carefully followed my doctrine, manner of life, purpose, faith, longsuffering, love, perseverance, persecutions, afflictions, which happened to me at Antioch, at Iconium, at Lystra—what persecutions I endured. And out of them all the Lord delivered me. Yes, and all who desire to live godly in Christ Jesus will suffer persecution. But evil men and impostors will grow worse and worse, deceiving and being deceived. But you must continue in the things which you have learned and been assured of, knowing from whom you have learned them, and that from childhood you have known the Holy Scriptures, which are able to make you wise for salvation through faith which is in Christ Jesus.

All Scripture is given by inspiration of God, and is profitable for doctrine, for reproof, for correction, for instruction in righteousness, that the man of God may be complete, thoroughly equipped for every good work.

Why does Paul remind Timothy of the many persecutions he endured? What does his willingness to go through these trials say about his belief in the message he was proclaiming?

What does Paul say that Timothy should do so that he is not taken in by evil men and impostors? From whom did Timothy learn the truth that he holds?

What does Paul say about the authority of Scripture? How does this serve as a test to determine whether the Word of God is true ?

Watch

Play the video for session six. As you watch, use the following outline to record any thoughts or concepts that stand out to you.

Notes

We can know the Old Testament we have today is reliable because of the detailed process the scribes in Israel went through to ensure the copies they were making *completely* matched the original (a detailed process that often took two to three years to complete).

Some people claim that certain non-canonical books should be included in the Bible (like the Gospel of Judas, the Gospel of Mary, the Gospel of Thomas, and the Gospel of Philip). However, most of these books were written after the first-century and thus were not eyewitness accounts.

The list of alleged contradictions to the Bible has grown shorter over time. As you examine the evidence, there are consistently reasonable explanations to all of these objections.

Evil and suffering is a huge issue that cause many people today to wrestle with God's goodness. But in Genesis 50:20, we are reminded that God works all things—even those things meant for evil—for good. This truth continually plays out through Scripture and in our lives.

Whenever you have doubts, it is important not to bury or ignore them. Talk to others, ask experts, and commit to finding an answer by examining the evidence.

The ultimate purpose of apologetics is not to know truth but to know how that truth applies to your life. Apologetics should shape your relationship with God, others, and yourself.

TIMELINE OF TRUE ORTHODOXY

- AD 33: Jesus dies and rises from the dead.

- AD 40s–60s: Paul writes letters to various churches; orthodoxy is pervasive and mainstream; churches are organized around a central message; undeveloped heresies begin to emerge; Scripture, schooling, singing, and sacraments teach core theology along with emerging early orthodox writings circulating in the churches.

- AD 60s–90s: The Gospels and the rest of the New Testament are written and continue to propagate the orthodoxy that preceded them; orthodoxy continues to be pervasive and mainstream; heresies are still undeveloped.

- AD 90s–130s: The New Testament writers pass from the scene; the apostolic fathers emerge and continue to propagate the orthodoxy that preceded them; orthodoxy is still pervasive and mainstream; heresies begin to organize but remain relatively undeveloped.

- AD 130s–200s: The apostolic fathers die out; subsequent Christian writers continue to propagate orthodoxy that preceded them; orthodoxy is still pervasive and mainstream, but various forms of heresy emerge; these heresies, however, remain subsidiary to orthodoxy and remain variegated.

- AD 200s–300s: Orthodoxy is solidified in the creeds, but various forms of heresy continue to rear their heads; orthodoxy, however, remains pervasive and mainstream.[3]

Discuss

Take a few minutes with your group members to discuss what you just watched and explore these concepts in Scripture.

1. During the teaching, Josh discussed how it took scribes two to three years to create a duplicate scroll using a process that included more than 4,000 built-in regulations to assure accuracy. Does this increase your confidence in the reliability of the Old Testament that we have today? Why or why not?

2. Why do you think the topic of the "secret gospels" is so popular in novels and movies (such as *The Da Vinci Code*)? After today's session, what is one tool you have learned for examining or questioning these supposed lost documents?

3. Josh and Sean offered several reasons for the alleged contradictions in the Bible. What is one that particularly stood out to you? Why that one?

4. Josh discussed how in his own life, he can now see how God used everything—even the painful situations—for his ultimate good. What are some ways that God has used painful experiences for good in your life? How have you been able to relate to others and help them as a result of your own experiences?

5. Have you ever felt guilty for having doubts about events or teachings mentioned in the Bible or in Christianity? How will you approach those feelings—and questions—differently now?

6. How has your understanding of apologetics shifted since the beginning of this study? What is the main difference that this change will have on your life?

Respond

C. S. Lewis was once an atheist who believed evil disproved the existence of God. But on deeper reflection, he changed his mind, stating, "My argument against God was that the universe seemed so cruel and unjust. But how had I got this idea of *just* and *unjust*? A man does not call a line crooked unless he has some idea of a straight line. What was I comparing the universe with when I called it unjust?"[4] The existence of evil ends up being an argument *for* God, because if there is such a thing as objective good, it means there must be a God. Today, close out your time by selecting two passages from the list below, and then write down what it says to you about God's goodness and love for the lost in this world.

Passage	What This Says About God's Goodness and Love
Psalm 34:8, 15–17	

Passage	What This Says About God's Goodness and Love
Matthew 5:43–48	
Luke 15:4–7	
Luke 19:6–10	
John 3:16–17	
Romans 3:23–26	
James 1:16–18	
1 John 1:5–7	

Pray

Wrap up your time by taking a few moments to pray together. Here are a few ideas of what you could pray about based on the topics of this session:

- Ask God for boldness in your beliefs *and* the humility to always seek the truth above being right.
- Ask God to help you with any doubts or fears you have about him.
- Pray to be a "relational apologist" who shares with others from a heart of love.
- Thank God that you can always rely on his Word to be your guide.
- Ask God to help you reveal the truth of his goodness to others in your life.

FINAL PERSONAL STUDY

Reflect on the material you've covered this week by engaging in any or all of the following activities. Each day offers a short reading from *Evidence That Demands a Verdict*, along with a few reflection questions to take you deeper into the theme of this week's study. Journal or write down your thoughts after each question. Share with your group leader or group members in the upcoming weeks any key points or insights that stood out to you.

❶ The Scribal Approach to Scripture
Evidence That Demands a Verdict, pages 97–98

When it comes to the evidence for why we can trust the reliability of the Old Testament, we need to look at how the scribes in Israel approached the serious task of transmitting Scripture. Paul D. Wegner, professor of Old Testament studies, notes:

> From at least the first century AD onward the proto-[Masoretic Text] was generally copied by well-trained, professional scribes who were meticulous in their work. Jewish writings mention that the temple employed correctors (*meggihim*) who scrutinized the scrolls to safeguard their precision. From about AD 100 to 300 a second group of scribes arose, called the Tannaim (*tannaim*), or 'repeaters' (i.e., teachers), who began copying their traditions shortly after the beginning of the Christian era."[5]

Wegner adds that sometime between 100 BC to AD 400, meticulous rules were developed to preserve the Old Testament text in synagogue scrolls:

- Only parchments from clean animals were allowed; these were to be joined together with thread from clean animals.
- Each written column of the scroll was to have no fewer than forty-eight and no more than sixty lines whose breadth must consist of thirty letters.
- The page was first to be lined, from which the letters were to be suspended.
- The ink was to be black, prepared according to a specific recipe.
- No word or letter was to be written from memory.
- There was to be the space of a hair between each consonant and the space of a small consonant between each word, as well as several other spacing rules.
- The scribe must wash himself entirely and be in full Jewish dress before beginning to copy the scroll.
- He could not write the name Yahweh with a newly dipped brush, nor could he take notice of anyone, even a king, while writing this sacred name.[6]

Later, an entire treatise was devoted to the proper procedure for preparing a sacred scroll and included even more rules intended to assure an accurate text. Given all of these precautions on the part of the scribes, we can be sure that the Bible was transmitted during this time period with great precision and accuracy.

Among the professional scribes, what was the role of the correctors (*meggihim*)?

What was the role of the second group of scribes, called the Tannaim (*tannaim*), or "repeaters" (i.e., teachers)?

Meticulous rules were developed to preserve the Old Testament text in synagogue scrolls. What is one rule that you find fascinating? What stands out to you about this one?

Note the rule that stated a scribe had to "wash himself entirely and be in full Jewish dress before beginning to copy the scroll." Why do you think this rule was necessary?

Do you feel more confident in the accuracy of the Old Testament text based on the information in today's reading? Why or why not?

② Jesus' View of the Old Testament
Evidence That Demands a Verdict, page 121

It is undeniable that Jesus considered the writings of the Old Testament as both inspired by God and authoritative for community decisions. James C. Vanderkam, a professor of Hebrew Scriptures, notes that in Matthew 19:3–9, we read of a dispute between Jesus and the Pharisees over the issue of divorce. Vanderkam notes how we can use this passage as an object lesson to demonstrate Jesus' regard for the authoritative nature of Old Testament Scripture:

> It is evident from the ways in which the encounters are recorded that both Jesus and his opponents knew and relied upon the scriptures as determinative in disputes. . . .

There is much to weigh in this passage, but the point relevant here is that both the Pharisees and Jesus assume the question they are discussing is to be answered from the scriptures—something so obvious that no one in the scene comments on it or raises a question about it. The books to which they appeal are in the Torah—Genesis and Deuteronomy—and both sides accept the authority of those books and are able to produce relevant data from them as needed.[7]

Clearly, Jesus viewed the Old Testament writings as authoritative because he believed they were the inspired words of God, spoken through Moses. Other passages in the Gospels indicate Jesus believed Moses was the final authority behind the Torah, while also equally affirming the authority of the Major and Minor Prophets.

Read Matthew 4:1–11. How did Jesus quote the Old Testament in this encounter?

Read Matthew 5:21–32 and compare that passage with Exodus 20:13–24 and Deuteronomy 24:1. What is Jesus quoting each time he states, "You have heard that is was said . . ." What does this tell you about the way Jesus viewed the authority of the Old Testament?

Read Matthew 19:3–9. What practical issue were Jesus and the Pharisees discussing?

What did the parties rely on to resolve the dispute? What does this tell you about the way in which both Jesus and the Pharisees viewed the Old Testament Scripture?

Read Matthew 5:17–18. What did Jesus say about the "Law" and the "Prophets" (the Old Testament)? What did Jesus see as his role?

How do you think Jesus would describe the role of Moses and other major and minor prophets in the development of Old Testament Scripture?

❸ Early Church's View of the Old Testament
Evidence That Demands a Verdict, pages 122–123

The New Testament authors and the early Christian church also viewed the Old Testament as authoritative. According to Lee Martin McDonald, a professor of New Testament, "The Christians believed that the whole story of God's plans and purposes for Israel developed in the Old Testament Scriptures had reached its completion in the life and work of Jesus. The New Testament writers saw continuity in what they were describing, presenting, or advocating with the ancient Jewish Scriptures. They fully accepted them as the authoritative word of God."[8]

Based on the evidence we have available, it is thus reasonable to conclude: (1) the text of the Hebrew Bible was copied with a high degree of accuracy from the time of the first century to our present day; (2) the identifiable variants between the primary textual traditions bear little significance to the core theological truths; and (3) Jesus, the New Testament authors, and the early Christian church all viewed the Old Testament as inspired by God, originally written by or spoken through the prophets, and accurately transmitted through the generations to the time of Jesus himself.

In the words of the Chicago Statement of Biblical Inerrancy, "No translation is or can be perfect, and all translations are an additional step away from the *autographa* [original]. Yet the verdict of linguistic science is that English-speaking Christians, at least, are exceedingly well served in these days with a host of excellent translations and have no cause for hesitating to conclude that the true Word of God is within their reach."[9]

What was the early church's view of the Old Testament writings?

Read Galatians 4:21–31. The apostle Paul frequently referred to stories and passages in the Old Testament. What story did he cite in this passage? What details did he highlight?

How did Paul use that story to make a point about the Old Covenant (Hagar/Ishmael) and the New Covenant (Sarah/Isaac)?

Read Hebrews 1:1–4. How did this author view the Old Testament? What did he say had changed now that Jesus had come into the world?

The New Testament writers saw continuity in what they were describing, presenting, or advocating with the ancient Jewish Scriptures. Do you think modern Christians embrace this same view of the Old Testament? Explain your response.

❹ Gnosticism Versus Orthodoxy
Evidence That Demands a Verdict, pages 124–127

In 1945, a collection of ancient manuscripts was found in Egypt near the village of Nag Hammadi. Among the discovered texts was the Gospel of Thomas. Upon its discovery, scholars realized three fragments in Greek had already been found in Oxyrhynchus, Egypt, in the 1890s, with the earliest fragment being dated to around AD 200. The discovery of these ancient texts prompted some scholars to speculate about why these were excluded from the New Testament canon and how they would have transformed the way we view Jesus and Christianity.

In his popular novel *The Da Vinci Code,* Dan Brown argues that the creation of the Bible was political and that those in power in the early church purposely excluded certain books from the canon. In other words, Christians in the church today have accepted a particular point of view based on what they think is reliable knowledge, but their beliefs actually consist of what was foisted on them by early church leaders. Brown's argument assumes this political dynamic is the way beliefs develop and applies it to the history of Christianity. This would mean there is no real orthodox Christianity, but just one form of Christianity that won out over the other.

Many of these noncanonical texts in question are categorized as *gnostic*. Broadly speaking, Gnosticism was centered on knowledge (or *gnosis*). A gnostic was dedicated to searching for secret teachings and hidden wisdom, so gnostic Christians focused less on Jesus as Savior and more on Jesus as a teacher of wisdom. This is because a basic tenet of Gnosticism was matter-spirit dualism, meaning that matter is inherently evil—and so irredeemable. Only spirit can be redeemed. Thus, Gnostics denied a bodily resurrection. They held to a *docetic* view of Jesus—that, as God, Jesus did not really have a physical body but only seemed to be human.

So, did this form of Christianity just lose out to the version of Christianity today that we consider orthodox? Esteemed historian Philip Jenkins says no: "Far from being the alternative voices of Jesus' first followers, most of the lost gospels should rather be seen as the writings of much later dissidents who broke away from an already established orthodox church. . . . We have a good number of genuinely early documents of Christian antiquity from before 125, long before the hidden gospels were composed, and these give us a pretty consistent picture of a church which is already hierarchical and liturgical, which possesses an organized clergy, and which is very sensitive to matters of doctrinal orthodoxy."[10]

How did the discovery of ancient texts at Nag Hammadi fuel the debate about what should be considered "orthodox" in Christianity?

What claim did Dan Brown imply in *The Da Vinci Code*? What does this argument assume?

What did the Gnostics focus on most in their version of Christianity? How was this different from orthodox Christianity?

The Gnostics believed all matter in the world is inherently evil and thus irredeemable, which led them to reject the bodily resurrection of Christ. What alternate belief did they hold?

How can you be sure that orthodox Christianity didn't just "win out" over an alternate form of Christianity (Gnosticism)?

❺ The "Lost" Gospels
Evidence That Demands a Verdict, pages 127–128, 132–134, 136–137, 139

Some of the most frequently argued-for extra-canonical writings include the Gospel of Thomas, the Gospel of Peter, and the Gospel of Mary. We will look at the content of each of these manuscripts and determine why they should not be included in the New Testament canon.

The Gospel of Thomas, which is basically a collection of 114 sayings attributed mostly to Jesus, is the most hotly debated of all noncanonical gospels. But the evidence reveals that its content *depends* on the canonical gospels. Such dependence—as well as the Gnostic elements that are prevalent within the text—discounts it as being an early and reliable source of information about the historical Jesus. And though some want to theorize an earlier version of Thomas, there is no objective evidence of such an ancient core.

The Gospel of Peter, first discovered in 1886 in Egypt, contains fantastic elements in comparison with the four canonical Gospel accounts of the resurrection, such as giant angels escorting Jesus from the tomb along with a cross that speaks. New Testament scholar Craig Evans concludes, "The evidence strongly suggests that the [Gospel of Peter] fragment is a late work, not an early work, even if we attempt to find an earlier substratum, gratuitously shorn of imagined late additions. . . . Given its fantastic features and coherence with late traditions, it is not advisable to make use of this Gospel fragment for Jesus research."[11]

The Gospel of Mary, discovered in the late nineteenth century, relates the story of Mary Magdalene recalling to the disciples the teachings Jesus had given to her. The idea that Jesus and Mary were lovers is fueled by this document, which says that Mary was "much loved by the Savior, as no other woman." However, according to biblical scholar C. M. Tuckett, this manuscript also draws heavily on the earlier canonical Gospels. Tuckett concludes, "Given the nature of the parallels that seem to exist, and the fact that some of the parallels involve at times redactional elements on the side of the (later to become) canonical texts, it seems likely that the Gospel of Mary is primarily a witness to the later, developing tradition generated by these texts, and does not provide independent witness to early Jesus tradition itself."[12]

These extracanonical gospels, and all the others besides, show evidence of late dating and dependence on the Gospels. Therefore, we should hold with confidence that Matthew, Mark, Luke, and John are the only true Gospels that give us accurate information about Christ.

Why do you think that so many people are fascinated with these Gnostic "lost Gospels"?

The Gospel of Thomas is the most hotly debated of all noncanonical gospels. But why should it not be included in the New Testament canon?

The Gospel of Peter contains many fantastic elements not found in the canonical Gospels. What are the reasons why it should not be included in the New Testament?

The Gospel of Mary contributed to the assertion that Jesus and Mary were lovers. But why should it not be included in the New Testament canon?

Given the evidence, how do you know that Matthew, Mark, Luke, and John are the oldest and most reliable narratives about the life, ministry, death, and resurrection of Jesus?

Leader's Guide

Thank you for your willingness to lead your group through this important study. What you have chosen to do is valuable and will make a great difference in the lives of others. The rewards of being a leader are different from those of participating, and we hope that as you lead you will find your own walk with Jesus deepened by this experience.

Evidence That Demands a Verdict: Jesus and the Gospels is a six-session study built around video content and small-group inter-action. As the group leader, just think of yourself as the host of a dinner party. Your job is to take care of your guests by managing all the behind-the-scenes details so that when everyone arrives, they can just enjoy time together.

As the group leader, your role is not to answer all the questions or reteach the content—the video, book, and study guide will do most of that work. Your job is to guide the experience and cultivate your small group into a kind of teaching community. This will make it a place for members to process, question, and reflect—not receive more instruction.

Before your first meeting, make sure everyone in the group gets a copy of the study guide. This will keep everyone on the same page and help the process run more smoothly. If some group members are unable to purchase the guide, arrange it so that people can share the resource with other group members. Giving everyone access to all the material will position this study to be as rewarding an experience as possible. Everyone should feel free to write in his or her study guide and bring it to group every week.

Setting Up the Group

You will need to determine with your group how long you want to meet each week so that you can plan your time accordingly. Generally, most groups like to meet for either ninety minutes or two hours, so you could use one of the following schedules:

Section	90 Minutes	120 Minutes
WELCOME (members arrive and get settled)	5 minutes	15 minutes
SHARE (discuss one or more of the opening questions for the session)	10 minutes	15 minutes
READ (discuss the questions based on the Scripture reading for the week)	10 minutes	15 minutes
WATCH (watch the teaching material together and take notes)	30 minutes	20 minutes
DISCUSS (discuss the Bible study questions you selected ahead of time)	30 minutes	40 minutes
RESPOND / PRAY (complete the individual closing exercise, pray together as a group, and dismiss)	5 minutes	15 minutes

As the group leader, you'll want to create an environment that encourages sharing and learning. A church sanctuary or formal classroom may not be as ideal as a living room, because those locations can feel formal and less intimate. No matter what setting you choose, provide enough comfortable seating for everyone, and, if possible, arrange the seats in a semicircle so everyone can see the video easily. This will make transition between the video and group conversation more efficient and natural.

Also, try to get to the meeting site early so you can greet participants as they arrive. Simple refreshments create a welcoming atmosphere and can be a wonderful addition to a group study evening. You may also want to consider offering childcare to couples with children who want to attend. Finally, be sure your media technology is working properly. Managing these details up front will make the rest of your group experience flow smoothly and provide a welcoming space in which to engage the content of *Evidence That Demands a Verdict.*

Starting the Group Time

Once everyone has arrived, it's time to begin the group. Here are some simple tips to make your group time healthy, enjoyable, and effective.

First, begin the meeting with a short prayer and remind the group members to put their phones on silent. This is a way to make sure you can all be present with one another and with God. Next, give each person a few minutes to respond to the questions in the "Share" and "Read" sections. This won't require as much time in session one, but beginning in session two, people will need more time to share their insights from their personal studies. Usually, you won't answer the discussion questions yourself, but you should go first with the "Share" and "Read" questions, answering briefly and with a reasonable amount of transparency.

At the end of session one, invite the group members to complete the between-sessions personal studies for that week. Explain that you will be providing some time before the video teaching next week for anyone to share insights. Let them know sharing is optional, and it's no problem if they can't get to any of the between-sessions activities some weeks. It will still be beneficial for them to hear from the other participants and learn about what they discovered.

Leading the Discussion Time

Now that the group is engaged, it's time to watch the video and respond with some directed small-group discussion. Encourage all the group members to participate in the discussion, but make sure they know they don't have to do so. As the discussion progresses, you may want to follow up with comments such as, "Tell me more about that," or, "Why did you answer that way?" This will allow the group participants to deepen their reflections and invite meaningful sharing in a nonthreatening way.

Note that you have been given multiple questions to use in each session, and you do not have to use them all or even follow them in order. Feel free to pick and choose questions based on either the needs of your group or how the conversation is flowing. Also, don't be afraid of silence. Offering a question and allowing up to thirty seconds of silence is okay. It allows people space to think about how they want to respond and also gives them time to do so.

As group leader, you are the boundary keeper for your group. Do not let anyone (yourself included) dominate the group time. Keep an eye out for group members who might be tempted to "attack" folks they disagree with or try to "fix" those having struggles. These kinds of behaviors can derail a group's momentum, so they need to be steered in a different direction. Model active listening and encourage everyone in your group to do the same. This will make your group time a safe space and create a positive community.

The group discussion leads to a closing time of individual reflection and prayer. Encourage the participants to take a few moments to review what they've learned during the session and write down their thoughts to the "Respond" section. This will help them cement the big ideas in their minds as you close the session. Conclude by having the participants break into smaller groups of two to three people to pray for one another.

Thank you again for taking the time to lead your group. You are making a difference in the lives of others and having an impact on the kingdom of God!

Endnotes

Session One: Why Is Evidence Important for Faith?

1. Friedrich Nietzche, *Daybreak: Thoughts on the Prejudices of Morality* (New York: Cambridge University Press, 1997), first published in 1881.
2. Lee Strobel, *The Case for Christ* (Grand Rapids, MI: Zondervan, 2004), p. 244.
3. Portions of the text for this opening section were adapted from the session 1 video teaching by Josh McDowell and Sean McDowell and from pages xlviii and xxxix in *Evidence That Demands a Verdict*.
4. Adapted from pages xxxiii–xxxvi in *Evidence That Demands a Verdict*.
5. Clark Pinnock, "Apologetics," in *New Dictionary of Theology*, edited by Sinclair B. Ferguson, David F. Wright, and J. I. Packer (Downers Grove, IL: InterVarsity Press, 2000), p. 36.
6. *Argumentum a fortiori* refers to drawing a conclusion that is inferred to be even more certain than the one just drawn. For example, if teaching English grammar to a native speaker is difficult, then *a fortiori*, teaching English grammar to a nonnative speaker will be even more challenging. See "*a fortiori*," *Merriam-Webster Dictionary*, https://www.merriam-webster.com/dictionary/a%20fortiori.
7. *Reductio ad absurdum* arguments disprove a proposition by showing the absurdity to which it would lead if carried to its logical conclusion. For example, if a child is in trouble and claims "but all my friends were doing it," a parent would show the absurdity of the argument by stating, "If all your friends were jumping off a bridge, would you do that too?" See "*reductio ad absurdum*," *Merriam-Webster Dictionary*, https://www.merriam-webster.com/dictionary/reductio%20ad%20absurdum.
8. Douglas Groothuis, "Jesus: Philosopher and Apologist," in Christian Research Journal 25, no. 2 (2002), http://www.equip.org/article/jesus-philosopher-and apologist/.
9. Os Guinness, *Fool's Talk: Recovering the Art of Christian Persuasion* (Downers Grove, IL: InterVarsity Press, 2015), pp. 15–16.
10. Clark Pinnock, *Set Forth Your Case* (Nutley, NJ: The Craig Press, 1967), pp. 6–7.
11. Craig Hazen, "Christianity in a World of Religions," in *Passionate Conviction: Contemporary Discourses On Christian Apologetics*, edited by Paul Copan and William Lane Craig (Nashville, TN: B&H Academic, 2007), p. 144.
12. Dallas Willard, *The Allure of Gentleness: Defending the Faith in the Manner of Jesus* (New York: HarperCollins, 2015), p. 4.

Session Two: Is There Such a Thing as Truth?

1. Stewart E. Kelly, *Truth Considered and Applied: Examining Postmodernism, History, and Christian Faith* (Nashville, TN: B&H Publishing Group, 2011), p. 267.
2. Portions of the text for this opening section were adapted from the session 2 video teaching by Josh McDowell and Sean McDowell and from pages 605–607 in *Evidence That Demands a Verdict*.

3. Ravi Zacharias, *Can Man Live Without God?* (Nashville, TN: Thomas Nelson, 1994), page 93.

4. Douglas Groothuis, *Truth Decay: Defending Christianity Against the Challenges of Postmodernism* (Downers Grove, IL: InterVarsity Press, 2000), p. 64

5. Wayne Grudem, *Systematic Theology: An Introduction to Biblical Doctrine* (Grand Rapids, MI: Zondervan, 1994), p. 568.

6. Sean McDowell, *Ethix: Being Bold in a Whatever World* (Nashville, TN: B&H Publishing Group, 2006), pp. 28–29.

7. Ibid., p. 29.

8. Paul Copan, *True for You, But Not for Me* (Minneapolis, MN: Bethany House, 1998), p. 27.

9. Francis J. Beckwith and Gregory Koukl, *Relativism: Feet Firmly Planted in Mid-Air* (Grand Rapids, MI: Baker Books, 1998), pp. 20, 22.

10. J. P. Moreland, "Postmodernism and Truth," in *Reasons for Faith: Making a Case for the Christian Faith*, edited by Norman L. Geisler and Chad V. Meister (Wheaton, IL: Crossway Books, 2007), pp. 113–114.

11. Moreland, *Love Your God with All Your Mind* (Carol Stream, IL: NavPress, 1997), p. 140.

12. Ibid., pp. 140–141.

Session Three: Is the New Testament Reliable?

1. Bart D. Ehrman, "The Historical Reliability of the New Testament," interview with The Best Schools, https://thebestschools.org/special/ehrman-licona-dialogue-reliability-new-testament/bart-ehrman-interview/.

2. Portions of the text for this opening section were adapted from the session 3 video teaching by Josh McDowell and Sean McDowell and from pages 42, 46, 68, 76, and 688 in *Evidence That Demands a Verdict*.

3. Donald A. Hagner, "The New Testament, History, and the Historical-Critical Method," in *New Testament Criticism and Interpretation*, edited by David Alan Black and David S. Dockery (Grand Rapids, MI: Zondervan, 1991), pp. 73–74.

4. F. F. Bruce, *The Books and the Parchments: How We Got Our English Bible*, revised edition, (Old Tappan, NJ: F. H. Revell, 1984), p. 86.

5. Ibid.

6. Ralph Earle, *How We Got Our Bible* (Grand Rapids, MI: Baker Book House, 1971), p. 33.

7. Michael J. Kruger, *The Question of Canon: Challenging the Status Quo in the New Testament Debate* (Downers Grove, IL: InterVarsity Press Academic, 2013), pp. 51–52.

8. Ibid., p. 62.

9. Ibid., p. 70.

10. John W. Montgomery, "Evangelicals and Archaeology," *Christianity Today*, August 16, 1968, p. 29.

11. Montgomery, *History and Christianity* (Downers Grove, IL: InterVarsity Press, 1971), pp. 34–35.

12. Richard Bauckham, *Jesus and the Eyewitnesses: The Gospels as Eyewitness Testimony* (Grand Rapids, MI: Eerdmans, 2006), pp. 73–74.

13. Montgomery, *History and Christianity*, p. 26.

14. Norman L. Geisler and William E. Nix, *A General Introduction to the Bible*, revised and expanded edition (Chicago, IL: Moody Press, 1986), p. 386.

15. Daniel B. Wallace, Lecture at Discover the Evidence, Dallas, TX, December 6, 2013.

16. Bruce M. Metzger and Bart D. Ehrman, *The Text of the New Testament: Its Transmission, Corruption, and Restoration*, fourth edition (Oxford University Press, 2005), p. 126;

compare J.H. Greenlee, *Introduction to New Testament Textual Criticism* (Grand Rapids, MI: Eerdmans, 1964, 1977), p. 54.

17. Craig Blomberg, quoted in Lee Strobel, *The Case for Christ: A Journalist's Personal Investigation of the Evidence for Jesus* (Grand Rapids, MI: Zondervan, 1998), p. 66.

18. Robert E. Van Voorst, *Jesus Outside the New Testament: An Introduction to the Ancient Evidence* (Grand Rapids, MI: Eerdmans, 2000), p. 39

19. Tacitus, *Annals* 15.44, quoted in John P. Meier, *A Marginal Jew: Rethinking the Historical Jesus*, vol. 1, New Anchor Yale Bible Reference Library (New York: Doubleday, 1991), pp. 89–90.

20. Michael R. Licona, *The Resurrection of Jesus: A New Historiographical Approach* (Downers Grove, IL: IVP Academic, 2010), p. 235.

21. Paul R. Eddy and Gregory A. Boyd, *The Jesus Legend: A Case for the Historical Reliability of the Synoptic Jesus Tradition* (Grand Rapids, MI: Baker Academic, 2007), p. 184.

22. Josephus, "Concerning Albinus Under Whose Procuratorship James Was Slain; as Also What Edifices Were Built by Agrippa," *Antiquities of the Jews*, book XX, chapter 9.

Session Four: Did Jesus Actually Rise from the Dead?

1. N. T. Wright, *The Resurrection of the Son of God* (Minneapolis, MN: Fortress Press, 2003), p. 33.

2. Portions of the text for this opening section were adapted from the session 4 video teaching by Josh McDowell and Sean McDowell and from pages 233–235 in *Evidence That Demands a Verdict*.

3. Wright, *The Resurrection of the Son of God*, p. 695.

4. Ibid., p. 31.

5. Ibid., p. 694.

6. Adrian Warnock, *Raised with Christ: How the Resurrection Changes Everything* (Wheaton, IL: Crossway, 2010), pp. 113–114.

7. Douglas Groothuis, *Christian Apologetics: A Comprehensive Case for Biblical Faith* (Downers Grove, IL: IVP Academic, 2011), p. 547.

8. Wright, "Christian Origins and the Resurrection of Jesus: The Resurrection of Jesus as a Historical Problem," *Sewanee Theological Review* 41, no. 2 (1998).

Session Five: Did Jesus Claim to Be God?

1. Walter W. Wessel and Mark L. Strauss, "Mark," *The Expositor's Bible Commentary*, vol. 9 (Grand Rapids, MI: Zondervan, 2010), pp. 825–826.

2. D. A. Carson, "Matthew," *The Expositor's Bible Commentary*, vol. 9 (Grand Rapids, MI: Zondervan, 2010), pp. 415–416.

3. Robert M. Price, "A Rejoinder to Josh McDowell's *Evidence That Demands a Verdict*: 'Jesus—God's Son' (1997)," accessed August 31, 2015, http://infidels.org/library/modern/ robert_price/son.html, Sec. 1B.

4. Bart Ehrman, *How Jesus Became God—the Exaltation of a Jewish Preacher from Galilee* (San Francisco: HarperOne, 2014), p. 44.

5. Portions of the text for this opening section were adapted from the session 5 video teaching by Josh McDowell and Sean McDowell and from page 173 in *Evidence That Demands a Verdict*.

6. Adapted from the session 5 video teaching by Josh McDowell.

7. Christopher A. Beetham, *Knowing the Bible: Colossians and Philemon, a 12-Week Study* (Wheaton, IL: Crossway, 2015), p. 30.

8. Peter Lewis, *The Glory of Christ* (London: Hodder & Stoughton, 1992), p. 241.
9. Stephen J. Wellum, "The Deity of Christ in the Apostolic Witness," in *The Deity of Christ*, edited by Christopher W. Morgan and Robert A. Peterson (Wheaton, IL: Crossway, 2011), p. 136.
10. Beetham, *Knowing the Bible*, p. 31.
11. C. S. Lewis, *Mere Christianity: A Revised and Amplified Edition, with a New Introduction, of the Three Books, Broadcast Talks, Christian Behaviour, and Beyond Personality* (San Francisco, CA: HarperSanFrancisco, 2001), pp. 55–56.

Session Six: How Do We Know the Bible Is Accurate?

1. Bart Ehrman, *Misquoting Jesus* (San Francisco: HarperOne, 2005), p. 248.
2. Portions of the text for this opening section were adapted from the session 6 video teaching by Josh McDowell and Sean McDowell and from page i in *Evidence That Demands a Verdict*.
3. Adapted from Andreas J. Köstenberger, Darrell L. Bock, and Josh D. Chatraw, *Truth in a Culture of Doubt: Engaging Skeptical Challenges of the Bible* (Nashville, TN: B&H Publishing Group, 2014), pp. 125–126.
4. C. S. Lewis, *Mere Christianity* (New York: Macmillan/Collier, 1952), p. 45.
5. Paul D. Wegner, *A Student's Guide to Textual Criticism of the Bible: Its History, Methods and Results* (Downers Grove, IL: IVP Academic, 2006), p. 73.)
6. Ibid.
7. James C. Vanderkam, *The Dead Sea Scrolls and the Bible* (Grand Rapids, MI: Wm. B. Eerdmans Publishing Co., 2012), pp. 53–54.
8. Lee Martin McDonald, *The Biblical Canon: Its Origin, Transmission, and Authority* (Grand Rapids, MI: Baker Academic, 2007) p. 207.
9. Chicago Statement of Biblical Inerrancy, quoted in Carl F. H. Henry, *Revelation and Authority*, vol. 4 (Waco, TX: Word Books, 1979), p. 218.
10. Philip Jenkins, *Hidden Gospels: How the Search for Jesus Lost Its Way* (Oxford University Press, 2001), pp. 12–13.
11. Craig A. Evans, *Fabricating Jesus: How Modern Scholars Distort the Gospels* (Downers Grove, IL: IVP Books, 2008), p. 85.
12. C. M. Tuckett, *The Gospel of Mary* (Oxford University Press, 2007), pp. 73–74.

ALSO AVAILABLE FROM JOSH McDOWELL AND SEAN McDOWELL

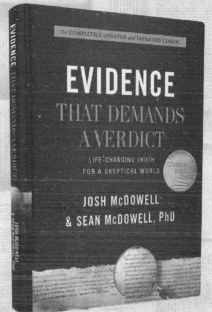

Available wherever books and ebooks are sold